SEIZED BY

SEIZED BY

Truth

READING THE BIBLE AS SCRIPTURE

JOEL B. GREEN

ABINGDON PRESS
Nashville

SEIZED BY TRUTH
READING THE BIBLE AS SCRIPTURE

This book is printed on acid-free paper.

Library of Congress Cataloging-in-Publication Data

Green, Joel B., 1956-
  Seized by truth : reading the Bible as Scripture / Joel B. Green.
    p. cm.
  Includes bibliographical references.
  ISBN 978-0-687-02355-4 (binding: pbk. : alk. paper)
  1. Bible—Hermeneutics. I. Title.
  BS476.G725 2007
  220.1—dc22

                                                                    2006032966

07 08 09 10 11 12 13 14 15 16—10 9 8 7 6 5 4 3 2 1
MANUFACTURED IN THE UNITED STATES OF AMERICA

CONTENTS

ACKNOWLEDGMENTS

My perspectives on the nature and interpretation of the Bible have developed slowly. Reared in a traditional Methodist church in West Texas, educated at Perkins School of Theology and the University of Aberdeen, and after some fifteen years of preaching regularly in congregations in Texas, Scotland, and California, I had long ago made peace with the apparent tensions between biblical authority and critical study of the Bible. I was fortunate to have before me such diverse exemplars as Mike Walker and Howard Marshall. Ongoing reflection has been prompted by ecclesial debates focusing on the authority of the Bible in doctrine and ethics, by ongoing engagement in preaching and teaching in congregations, by conversations with a number of students (both in Berkeley and at Asbury Theological Seminary), and by interactions with a wide array of persons in the area of theological hermeneutics. Lest the number quickly swell beyond reasonable proportions, I will resist the temptation to begin listing those persons by name—though I must record my gratitude to Dr. Chuck Gutenson and the Reverend Randy Shrauner, who commented on a draft of this book.

Impetus for this project came from Greg Glover, one-time Senior Academic Editor at Abingdon Press; it was he who urged me to pull together from sundry lectures and publications a book on the Bible as Scripture. I am grateful for Greg's initial suggestions, and for the ongoing encouragement I have received from Kathy Armistead, friend and development editor at Abingdon.

The lengthy and involved period of incubation of the perspectives and substance of this book include invited lectures and papers in a number of settings and a range of publications. I am grateful for opportunities for interaction on these concerns afforded me by invitations to give lectures in the context of several professional organizations, including Christian Theological Research Fellowship, Evangelical Theological Society, Institute of Biblical Research, Society of Biblical Literature (Southeastern Region), Society of Pentecostal Studies, and Wesleyan Theological Society; and the following institutions: Anderson University, Bethel College, College of the Ozarks, Furman University, North Park Theological Seminary, and Wheaton College. Although lacking any one-to-one correspondence with the chapters of this book, I have drawn on ideas developed in earlier publications, including: "Modernity, History, and the Theological Interpretation of the Bible," *Scottish Journal of Theology* 54 (2001): 308-29; "Reading the Bible as Wesleyans," *Wesleyan Theological Journal* 33 (1998): 116-29 (adapted in "Is There a Contemporary Wesleyan Hermeneutic?" in *Reading the Bible in Wesleyan Ways: Some Constructive Proposals* [ed. Barry Callen and Richard P. Thompson; Kansas City: Beacon Hill, 2004], 123-34); "Scripture and Theology: Failed Experiments, Fresh

Perspectives," *Interpretation* 56 (2002): 5-20; "Scripture in the Church: Reconstructing the Authority of Scripture for Christian Formation and Mission," in *The Future of Methodism: Trajectories into the Third Millennium* (ed. Paul Wesley Chilcote; Nashville: Abingdon Press, 2002), 38-51; "Practicing the Gospel in a Post-Critical World: The Promise of Theological Exegesis," *Journal of the Evangelical Theological Society* 47 (2004): 387-97; "Contribute or Capitulate? Wesleyans, Pentecostals, and Reading the Bible in a Postcolonial Mode," *Wesleyan Theological Journal* 39 (2004): 74-90; and "Hermeneutical Approaches to the Tradition (New Testament)," in *Eerdmans Commentary on the Bible* (ed. James D. G. Dunn and John W. Rogerson; Grand Rapids: Eerdmans, 2003), 972-88.

C H A P T E R O N E

READING THE BIBLE, READING SCRIPTURE

At one time people knew what it meant to read a text as scrip-
ture, but we no longer do, because this way of reading has,
since the late medieval and reformation periods, been dislocated
and obscured.[1]

For those of us who read the Bible from within the church these are astonishing words. True, there are many places where the Bible might be read quite apart from its religious significance. A statement published jointly by The Bible Literacy Project, Inc., and the First Amendment Center—endorsed by organizations as diverse as the People for the American Way Foundation, the Baptist Joint Committee on Public Affairs, and the Society of Biblical Literature—notes that educators widely agree that study about the Bible can be an important part of a complete education in courses such as literature and history. "Knowledge of biblical stories and concepts contributes to our understanding of literature, history, law, art, and contemporary society."[2] Encouraging study about the Bible in public schools, this document sketches possibilities for curriculum related to the Bible and literature, the Bible and history, and the Bible and world religions. As important as this project might be on its own terms, this is not reading the Bible as Scripture.

The case I want to make in this chapter is that the slogan that has driven critical study of the biblical materials—"Read the Bible as you would read any other book"—however helpful and well-intentioned, cannot on its own promote a reading of the Bible as Scripture. This way of engaging the Bible cannot sustain the people of God. This motto, I will urge, is not so much inappropriate as it is inadequate. It is not even the most important, first step to be taken.

An image may help. Most of us have woken too early, dressed in too little light, and found our blouse or shirt out of alignment: buttons in the wrong buttonholes. We did everything right, used good technique, placed each button carefully into and through the hole provided, but we started in the wrong place and therefore achieved an unwanted result. Attention to genre, the structure of an argument, the meaning of words and phrases, social background—we will turn to these concerns in due course, but they do not constitute "first things." What it means to embrace the Bible as Scripture and the nature of human formation and practices—these are first things. Coming at the question from several vantage points—including theological considerations, teaching and learning, reflections on history and historicism, and multidisciplinary perspectives on human formation—I will urge that we need to attend better to what we bring with us when we bring ourselves to the task of read-ing the Bible.

This Is the Word of God?

Reading the Bible is not necessarily the same thing as reading Scripture. More specifically, when we read the Bible we are not nec-essarily reading the Bible *as Scripture*. In some ways, this is an obvious truth, but we may still be surprised by it. At one level, this is the experience of many ordinary Christians who take up the Bible and read its words, then walk away unchanged, uninspired, and uncer-tain. This is the Word of God? What does it mean? Who can make sense of these words? Yet, millions of Americans gather week after week in homes, workplaces, and coffee shops to accomplish this very thing, to make sense of these words, to hear the voice of God speaking to them.[3] And, like annuals in the flower bed, new study Bibles and Bible study tools, promising clarity, wisdom, and inspiration, appear each summer in local bookshops.

> **Reading the Bible is not necessarily the same thing as reading Scripture.**

Ordinary Christians might be stunned to discover it, but it is no less true that the seminary-trained and the scholar share this common experience of dryness in the journey through the pages of the Bible. In fact, for those apprenticed in the ways of biblical scholarship dur-ing the last two centuries, the experience of distance between ancient text and faithful life is often even more pronounced. The arsenal available to those trained in the science of biblical scholarship may burgeon with a wider array of skills and critical methods, well-honed tools, and promising techniques, but these do not ensure that God's word will be any more near, or that it will be any more reverenced or observed. To many of us, this may seem counterintuitive. Why would greater skill not lead to greater understanding?

Our problems are several, but most debilitating are the traditions of knowing and learning that many of us take for granted. Yale University professor Robert J. Sternberg has observed, "Traditional education, and the intellectual and academic skills it provides, furnishes little protection against evil-doing or, for that matter, plain foolishness."[4] By "traditional," Sternberg refers to educational practices developed especially in the last century. These, he insists, are the educational goals that need revamping. However necessary academic skills may be, he observes, they are insufficient for persons committed to using their intelligence to seek a common good. Rather, he writes, we easily succumb to the temptation to confuse learning practical skills with gaining knowledge and mistake the amassing of facts with learning. How could we know so much and be so lacking in wisdom? Is it not because there is no simple line from the accumulation of data to the formation of a person?

In the same way, the exercise of reading the Bible, even reading according to accredited protocols and conventional procedures, need have no particular relationship to reading Scripture, even though both have to do with reading the same texts, the same pages. To refer to "Scripture" rather than "Bible" introduces a category difference in assumptions and aims, making it entirely possible, nowadays perhaps even probable, that a reading of the Bible will not be a reading of Scripture. From wildly diverse perspectives, the biblical scholar Robert Morgan and the theologian David Kelsey document what is at stake. Observing the competing interests occupying those who engage in interpreting the biblical materials, Morgan concludes that what we take the biblical texts to mean does not depend simply on the character of those texts, or on the nature of the methods we bring to the work of reading those texts. "Interpretation depends more on the interests of the interpreters," he claims, before observing that "the aims of biblical historians [i.e., scholars in the field of biblical studies] seem quite remote from those of Jews and Christians who interpret the Bible in the expectation of religious insight."[5] For his part, Kelsey writes, "To take biblical writings simply as 'texts' is, notoriously, not necessarily to take them as 'Christian scripture.'" To take biblical texts as Scripture has to do with the aim of Scripture, which, he insists, is to "shape persons' identities so decisively as to transform them."[6]

In short, "the Bible is Scripture" is first and foremost a theological statement. It draws attention to the origin, role, and aim of these texts in God's self-communication. It locates persons and a community of people, those who read the Bible as Scripture, on a particular textual map, a location possessing its own assumptions, values, and norms for guiding and animating particular

> **In short, "the Bible is Scripture" is first and foremost a theological statement.**

beliefs, dispositions, and practices that together constitute that people. Because of its priority in the generation and sustenance of the world it supports, Scripture also holds the potential for confirming or for reconfiguring the beliefs and commitments that orient our lives in the world.[7]

Knowing, Doing, Trusting

How, then, might we read the Bible as Scripture? It almost goes without saying that the solution would not be a dismissal of knowing the "stuff" of the Old and New Testaments. The solution to "traditional education," to recall Sternberg's words, is not to evacuate knowledge of the Bible's contents from our philosophies and practices of teaching and learning. Who among us would ever say that our problem is that too many of us know the Bible too well? We would more likely be tempted to join the choir of voices decrying biblical illiteracy. It comes as no surprise to most of us that Robert Wuthnow, one of our leading cultural analysts, has found that "a sizeable segment of the American public has moved away from the Bible as a source of spiritual insight."[8] Even so, even more troubling may be the inability of practicing Christians to answer basic

> **We cannot . . . confuse expertise in the game of Bible trivia with the kind of tacit knowledge that marks faithfulness to Christian Scripture.**

questions about the Bible's contents. Name the twelve tribes of Israel. Name the twelve apostles. Name the prophets that together make up the Book of the Twelve. There is something to be said for simply expanding our knowledge base concerning data from and about the Bible. Nevertheless, we cannot and must not confuse expertise in the game of Bible trivia with the kind of tacit knowledge that marks faithfulness to Christian Scripture.

Nor would the way forward be marked by the absence of methods and procedures for engaging biblical texts. Discipline in our work with these ancient books should not be discounted, since the biblical books, like any other writing we encounter, confront us with interpretive obstacles that must be negotiated in our quest for understanding. Some of these obstacles are so simple, so endemic to communication of all kinds, that we might overlook them:

- *Language is linear.* In the case of a painting by Van Gogh, for example, or Renoir, we experience the whole at once. This is not so with texts, whose "whole" is revealed to us one bit at a time, progressively, as we read from left to right (as in English, say, or Greek) or right to left (as in Hebrew). Were we to describe to someone else what we saw when we viewed Van Gogh's *The Church at Auvers*, we could do so only by introducing linearity into our experience of the painting: What to say first? Second? Similarly, narrative texts such as Exodus or Acts unveil the "mighty acts of God" not all at once, but in an ordered fashion. Reading further in a text, our insider knowledge expands, setting the stage for our understanding what will follow, at the same time that reading further clarifies in retrospect what seemed ambiguous early on. Reading the whole text and reading the text as a whole, together with attention to sequence, thus become nonnegotiable protocols for the competent interpreter.

- *Language is selective.* The less said, the more required of the interpreter, who must fill in the gaps. Writers today, say, a biographer or novelist, can go on and on, and often do, producing hundreds of pages by way of making the first president of the United States seem more like a living friend than a figure of the past, or by way of introducing us to the smells and sounds of a great battle in the Civil War. In such cases, readers are carried along for the ride. Caught in the cascade of interpretive detail, interpretive reflection on the part of the reader seems unnecessary. When the production of even a relatively short document such as Paul's Letter to the Galatians might take days, pass through repeated drafts, and in today's economy cost more than seven hundred dollars,[9] though, we might not be surprised that frugality of words was more the norm, with more work to be done by the interpreter. For letters in Roman antiquity, an authorized, letter-carrying emissary might "perform" the letter, reading it with gestures and changes of intonation to make clear how it was to be heard, and be otherwise counted on to assist with interpretive detail. With copies made and circulated more widely, however, communities of reading and hearing would need to expend more and more energy to make sense. Of course, many gaps occur because of shared assumptions between the writer and the authorial audience, creating even more interpretive obstacles for the twenty-first-century audience who is not so intimate with the first-century world.

- *Language is ambiguous.* Words and phrases typically carry multiple possible meanings, and these give rise to more uncertainties. Native English speakers are unlikely to confuse the dual meaning of *blue* in references to a *blue* mood and a *blue* sky, but persons for whom English is a second or third language may need some help. So we might be forgiven for wondering how the *kosmos* ("world") that God so loved (John 3:16) could also be the *kosmos* ("world") in this phrase: "Whoever desires to befriend the world proves to be God's enemy" (James 4:4, my translation). We need some work in lexical semantics to help us here.

- *Language is culturally embedded.* The Old Testament is in Hebrew (with a little Aramaic); the New Testament is in Greek. We know this, but the ease with which we accept these statements masks an important problem. With such an array of modern translations in English, the words of the Bible are readily accessible to us, so much so that we might and often do simply assume that its words, familiar to us in translation, also carry commonplace meaning from our world. Reading the Bible today in English, we imagine without a second thought that people in the ancient Mediterranean world experienced life much as we do. Too readily, we stumble over the reality that every reading of the Bible today is in some important sense an exercise in cross-cultural communication and understanding. The result is that we naturally recruit biblical texts in support of our own interests and practices.

More could be said, but hopefully enough has been said to show why procedures and protocols in interpretation are necessary.

But they are not enough. The best methods rightly used guarantee neither a Christian interpretation of the Bible nor a reading of the Bible as Christian Scripture. Paradoxically, they might even get in the way of a Christian interpretation of the Bible or a reading of the Bible as Scripture. Employing them as meaning-making machines, we might struggle with how so much hard work can result in so little payoff. This is especially true in a world such as ours that first divorces the practical from the theoretical and then elevates the practical ("Here's how . . .") and demonizes theory ("merely academic"); in a world such as ours that has had a century-long love affair with "technique," that prioritizes form over formation. In such

> **The best methods rightly used guarantee neither a Christian interpretation of the Bible nor a reading of the Bible as Christian Scripture.**

a world, we move quickly to method when there is something even more basic.

What is this something? Writing of "understanding" in her fantasy novel *The Telling*, Ursula K. LeGuin observes:

> One of the historians of Darranda said: *To learn a belief without belief is to sing a song without the tune.*
>
> A yielding, an obedience, a willingness to accept these notes as the right notes, this pattern as the true pattern, is the essential gesture of performance, translation, and understanding. The gesture need not be permanent, a lasting posture of the mind or heart; yet it is not false. It is more than the suspension of disbelief needed to watch a play, yet less than a conversion. It is a position, a posture in the dance.[10]

I will later argue that a temporary suspension of disbelief is not enough, that a full-blown conversion is needed, and warranted. But with uncommon wisdom, LeGuin starts us on the right path. This is because reading the Bible specifically as Scripture may include an interest in the voice of the Bible's human authors, but is unsatisfied with interests so narrowly defined. Reading the Bible as Scripture accords privilege to the role of this text in divine self-disclosure. Accordingly, to borrow from LeGuin, for Christians and Christian communities set on reading the Bible so as to hear God's address, "a yielding, an obedience, a willingness to accept these notes as the right notes, this pattern as the true pattern"—this "is the essential gesture of performance, translation, and understanding." Accordingly, more necessary than familiarity with ancient peoples and their cultures, more basic than learning the biblical languages, and more essential than good technique in interpretation are such dispositions and postures and gestures as acceptance, devotion,

Key theme

11

attention, and trust. Accordingly, we acknowledge and invite the ongoing work of Scripture's divine author as the One capable and desirous of authoring a community, the church, God's people: to call it into being, to sculpt this community and its people, to renew them.

The Great Divide

Such gestures or postures do not come naturally. Never mind our predilection to go our own way rather than live in a creaturely relationship to God and God's world. Never mind the lurking presence of sin that renders us unready and unwilling to place ourselves (or allow ourselves to be placed) like clay on the potter's wheel of God's word. We can recognize more simply how our inherited approaches to learning can work against us. Recalling memories of frogs in middle school science labs, a student once observed about the work of biblical interpretation, "First you have to kill it, then you can dissect it." Adopting basic instincts from the natural sciences, biblical scholars have learned to identify carefully what separates our worlds from the worlds to which the biblical materials give witness. That was they and this is we. That was there and this is here. That was then and this is now.

Exploring differences is important work. Who would confuse twenty-first-century Bakersfield, California, with ancient Jericho? Clothing, diet, travel, health care, wildlife, and a thousand other artifacts and habits distinguish these worlds. Exploring differences is important, not least because it carries with it the capacity to protect the Bible from captivity to modern opinions and categories. However, we cannot escape the fact that no approach more clearly separates the message of the Bible from those of us who turn to it for religious insight.[11]

Scientific methods objectify the text—that is, they turn the biblical materials into an object to be examined. They seek to secure the text's "difference," its primary quality of "not like us," in order to ensure that we do not read ourselves and our assumptions into the ancient text. Its world is not our world. Its ways are not our ways. Its presuppositions are not ours. We come to the biblical text from the outside. We come as visitors from another land. If we are concerned with applying the Bible to our lives, scientific approaches teach us to make safari into the Bible's strange world, capture the meaning that we find there, and transport it back to our world so as to display it and, if possible, to translate what we have learned about the past into contemporary idiom. For the scientific reader of the Bible, there is no inherent need to concern ourselves with the significance of the Bible for ourselves. It is sufficient to study these texts on their own terms, for their significance as cultural products in their own times. It is not only sufficient, but even preferable, since to come to these texts with "commitments" is to risk contamination of the evidence, turning the data toward our interests rather than allowing it to speak to us from its own interests. Either way, whether inviting or resisting contemporary application of the message of the Bible, the first methodological assumption and consequence is a great divide, a chasm separating biblical and contemporary faith.

The fissure separating ancient biblical text and contemporary faith is the result of tectonic shifts and their aftershocks over the last three centuries. Alister McGrath conveniently refers to the epicenter of this movement as the sense of "being condemned to history": "The confident and restless culture of the Enlightenment experienced the past as a burden, an intellectual manacle which inhibited freedom and stifled creativity."[12] Thus, as Carl E. Schorske writes:

> In most fields of intellectual and artistic culture, twentieth-century Europe and America learned to think without history. The very word 'modernism' has come to distinguish our lives and times from what had gone before, from history as a whole, as such. Modern architecture, modern music, modern science—all these have defined themselves not so much *out* of the past, indeed scarcely *against* the past, but detached from it in a new, autonomous cultural space.[13]

In the theological arena, interest in a theology without tradition resulted in perennial questions about the place of the study of the Bible in the seminary curriculum, just as the increasingly historical definition of the meaning of the biblical materials led to the segregation of "serious" biblical studies from issues of biblical authority and biblical relevance. In an op-ed piece posted in 2006, Michael Fox, professor of Hebrew at the University of Wisconsin, Madison, urged that faith-based study of the Bible is not scholarship; in fact, he says, "The best thing for Bible appreciation is [a] secular, academic, religiously-neutral hermeneutic."[14]

Put sharply, this massive shift is centered in the problematizing of "history." If, as is increasingly recognized, all knowledge is historically grounded, then we moderns should not be governed in our knowing by someone else's history, including the history of the biblical

14

materials themselves and the Christian tradition. How does this orientation impinge on biblical studies? It has led to the assumption that the only viable history within which to construe the meaning of biblical texts is the history within which those texts were generated—or the history to which those texts give witness. The results for Christian theology and preaching have often been disastrous, since it is difficult to construe the meaning for contemporary times of a biblical text whose meaning properly belongs to an ancient time.

Painting with the broadest of strokes, we can summarize by historical era three ways of relating biblical text and historical context. *Premodern perspectives* typically worked with the assumption that text and history were inseparable, or, when this relationship could not be taken for granted, that the history behind the text was not the sole or determinative factor in meaning making. Exegesis was not a task discrete from theology; rather, the hard-nosed work of premodern exegetes was the sermon, theological treatise, catechesis, and the like.

The *modern perspective* posits a purposeful segregation of "history" and "text." Here we learn that the history to which the biblical text gives witness and the biblical text that provides such a witness are not two expressions of the one reality. Prior to the onset of the Protestant Reformation in the 1500s and the rise of the "new science" in the 1600s, the universe, as Umberto Eco put it, was "nothing other than an emanative outpouring from the unknowable and unnamable One down to the furthest ramifications of matter," with every being functioning as "a synecdoche or metonymy of the

One."[15] If the entire sensible world is a book written by the hand of God, then all of nature serves together with the Bible as a combined witness to reveal the Divine Author. When Protestant interpretation of the Bible countered with its emphasis on the "literal sense," it followed only naturally that nature, too, would be examined along different lines. This new literalism distinguished between text and world by making each the focus of its own interpretive interests.[16] What is more, since in modern biblical studies interpretive privilege was accorded to the hard facts of history, the biblical text came to be regarded with critical suspicion. Biblical interpretation thus became a discipline of "validation" (when the biblical text is judged to represent historical events with accuracy) or "reconstruction" (when it is not).

More recently, some have migrated to forms of study for which there are no "facts," only "perspectives." Texts are sundered from the sociohistorical contexts within which they were generated, from those texts alongside which they reside within the biblical canon, from the traditions of interpretation that have grown up around them over these millennia, and from whatever interpretive constraints might have been suggested by the texts themselves. Because these impulses continue the modern agenda of sundering the present from the past, it is arguable whether these forms of study are only *late-modern*, and not yet *postmodern* after all.[17]

More to the point perhaps, in *postmodernism*, the icon of the neutral interpreter engaged in objective historical work, so central to the modern era, is shattered. Postmodernity denies the existence of a ledge of objective truth on which the reader might stand in order to

> **Postmodernity denies the existence of a ledge of objective truth on which the reader might stand in order to make value-free judgments.**

make value-free judgments in the enterprise of discerning or making meaning. To shift the metaphor, interpreters can no longer hide behind the veil of a presumed ideological neutrality.[18] Interestingly, although this new recognition of the "location" of the reader (and its influences on the interpretive task) has tended to turn its spotlight on issues of gender or economic status, the theological location of the reader is also reintroduced into the conversation, at least potentially. Space is thus cleared for construing biblical studies as "faith seeking understanding."

Responses to this evolving state of affairs have varied. Some have urged that academic study of the Bible has no place for religious concerns. Some have simply rejected serious biblical studies in favor of religious concerns. Others have embraced scientific methods, urging that we can and ought to derive "what it means" from "what it meant"—and, indeed, that the only way to know "what it means" is by first establishing "what it meant"—leading to a hermeneutical motto like this one: observation leads to interpretation, and interpretation to application.

From my vantage point, none of these responses has demonstrated much traction. The first and second capitulate to one side of the argument or the other, recognizing the chasm between biblical studies and faith, but refusing the possibility or need to engineer a bridge between them. The third attempts a bridge, but the resulting structure has proved difficult to traverse. Good examples are few; this response seems open only to the most talented, the most sure-footed among us.[19] The question I want to pose is not whether we ought to live on one side of the chasm or the other, or even how best to span the distance between them. Rather, I wonder why we must admit the chasm at all. Can we reconceive our work with the Bible as Scripture?

Whereas scientific exegesis has highlighted the historical chasm separating ancient text and contemporary readers, reading the Bible as Scripture focuses on whether we share (or refuse) the theological vision of the biblical text. Emphasis falls on our dispositions toward "standing under" (or toward "standing over") the Scriptures. Center stage belongs to those practices of engaging with Scripture that embody the reader's commitment to live faithfully (or not) before the God to whom the Scriptures witness. The first question, then, is not what separates us (language, diet, worldview, politics, social graces, and so forth) from the biblical authors, but whether we are ready to embrace the God to whom and the theological vision to which these writers bear witness.[20]

Prioritizing Formation

What aims and assumptions guide our engagement with the Bible as Scripture? What patterns of faith and thought operate at a pre-cognitive level, setting the compass for our interpretive work? By way of framing this question, let me garner help from the philosopher and social scientist Pierre Bourdieu. In his analysis of human agency and interactions, Bourdieu concerned himself with accounting for the practical competence of human agents and the social conditions within which those encounters take shape and find meaning. Developing a theory of practice, he gave special attention to the concept of *habitus*, those dispositions that incline agents to respond and act in certain ways without those actions and responses being ruled by external authorities or even coordinated by thoughtful decision making. These are patterns "of durable, transposable dispositions" that "generate and organize practices and representations that can be objectively adapted to their outcomes without presupposing a conscious aiming at ends or an express mastery of the operations necessary in order to attain them."[21]

Dispositions, then, are both "embodied history" and "embodied compass," internalized and so operative at a preconscious level. Practices grow out of the interplay of this "second nature" and specific social contexts. Adapting Bourdieu's model for our purposes, we can see how it has immediate implications for our thinking about Christian formation, which, then, would grow out of the interrelations among our patterns of faith and thought, our allegiances and commitments, and our practices. Why is this important? To start, it helps us map the chasm between the character of ethical discourse and formation in many churches and church-related institutions today, and in Christian Scripture. Whereas the church and its related institutions tend to focus on "moral acts," Scripture is far more concerned with shaping our imaginations, our patterns of thinking, which, inevitably, find expression in transformed commitments and practices. Behavior serves as a display case for our deepest commitments.

Two further observations: (1) This model suggests how our Scripture-formed patterns of thinking and acting might take different shapes—not because the words of Scripture have changed, but because the social contexts within which those words are read and put into play vary. (2) If dispositions give rise to behavior, the reverse is also true. Practices sculpt character. We can only do what we are, but, paradoxically, our becoming what we are is shaped by our practices. Thus, for example, the apostle Peter can call upon his audience to practice hospitality, to be good stewards of the grace of God, and to love without pretentiousness (1 Pet. 1:22; 4:8-10) both without regulating the precise form those practices might take and without concern for whether his audience feels like behaving in just these ways. Hospitality, stewardship, and unpretentious love—these dispositions will take varied forms appropriate to the needs and opportunities of particular community settings. Living out of Scripture-formed patterns is thus a matter of creative fidelity— "fidelity" in the sense that these patterns set the parameters of faithful performance, "creative" in the sense that life is too particular and unruly to be carefully scripted—but Christians can nonetheless be persons shaped by this pattern, and who navigate life accordingly. Such are the habits of the household of God, and those who practice them find that they become more and more that household, that community that embodies in its inner life the life of God.

The point, of course, is that our practices, including our engagement with the Bible, flow out of preunderstandings that are not often found under the microscope of scrutiny. These typically unacknowledged preunderstandings parade under the nontechnical label of "jumping to conclusions," what neuroscientists sometimes refer to as "filling in."[22] Various terms name the structures or patterns by which we "fill in"—*imagination* ("a basic image-schematic capacity for ordering our experience"[23] or "the power of taking something as something by means of meaningful forms, which are rooted in our history and have the power to disclose truths about life in the world"[24]), for example, or *conceptual schemes* (schemes that are at once *conceptual* [a way of seeing things], *conative* [a set of beliefs and values deeply shared within a community], and *action guiding* [we live according to its terms]).[25] We "make sense" in terms of imaginative structures or conceptual schemes that we implicitly take to be true, normal, and good.[26]

What is the source of these conceptual schemes, these patterns for ordering our lives and making sense of our experiences? We are formed in them, quite literally. The raw material might come by way of genetics, but the shaping, the sculpting, is left largely to years of interactions with our intimates, our family and friends, and whatever else we allow to fill our minds and occupy our attention. Happily for most of us, it is not the case that, once formed, always formed. Indeed, research has demonstrated that various psychotherapies, for example, can produce physiological changes in the brain, with the result that old forms of response are eclipsed by fresh patterns of response.[27] More generally, from birth, we are in the process of becoming, and this "becoming" is encoded in our brains by means of synaptic activity. In our first two years (and beyond), far more synapses are generated than are needed, so that in the first years of life and the last years of adolescence we experience a veritable explosion of mapping and remapping of brain circuitry. Those neural connections that are used are maintained and remodeled, while those that fall into disuse are eliminated. But fresh connections are generated in response to our experiences, even into adulthood, until the very moment of death.

My brain imposes structure on the data it receives from its sensory organs, contributing to a baseline conclusion that my sense of reality is both embodied and interpreted within the framework of my formation as a social being. My "perception" of the world is based in a network of ever-forming assumptions about my environment, and in a series of well-tested assumptions, shared by others with whom I associate, about "the way the world works." To a degree not often realized, then, *believing is seeing*.

Ambiguous data may present different hypotheses, but my mind disambiguates that data according to what I have learned to expect. That is, receiving information in the present, I make sense of this information in terms of the past, and on this basis calculate potential futures. In fact, patients who have experienced selected lesions to the brain demonstrate the inability to see what they cannot believe to be true,[28] just as those of us with unaffected brains operate normally with a strong hermeneutical bias on the basis of prior beliefs, so that we actually perceive stimuli when none are physically presented.[29] This is what "interpretation" does: it renders the significance of the present in terms determined by the past, and allows people to anticipate a future that flows out of the past. Of course, this does not mean that we are trapped in our beliefs, or that there is no reality outside of our subjective experience of it; rather, healthy minds perform tests incessantly to assess the relationship between perceptions and fresh sensory data. But this assumes that our minds can jump out of the deep ruts formed by years of traffic along familiar pathways. The miracle is that the horizons of our assumptions can be enlarged and transformed, and this is precisely the work of Christian Scripture.

These considerations underscore the importance of the church, that community within which we might be formed and transformed, and the Scriptures, that theological vision that incarnates itself in our ways of experiencing and interacting with the world around us. One way to think about the aims and assumptions guiding our reading of the Bible as Scripture, then, is to reflect on those patterns of thinking, believing, feeling, and behaving into which the church inducts (or ought to induct) its members. Another is to imagine what patterns promote the reading of these texts as Scripture.

> **The Scriptures are a theological vision that incarnates itself in our ways of experiencing and interacting with the world around us.**

Conclusion

Thus far, I have come at a singular argument from different perspectives. I have urged that what we have come to know about the mind and the brain underscores the potentially formative role of reading the Bible as Scripture within the church constituted by those Scriptures. From this perspective, Christian formation relates to the whole of who we are, our embodied lives, with Scripture taking on the role of sculptor, shaping our patterns of thinking, feeling, believing, and acting. I have urged that the practice of reading Scripture is both cause and effect of our formation as Christians among the community of God's people.

I have urged that to claim the Bible as Scripture is a theological statement that directs our attention to the origin, role, and aim of these texts in God's self-communication. As such, it assumes, at the same time that it invites and cultivates, certain commitments of the claimant and, even more so, of the community called into being by the God whose voice is heard in the Scriptures. These commitments are realized in a yielding, an obedience, a willingness to accept these patterns as the right ones, and in such dispositions and gestures as acceptance, devotion, attention, and trust. And I have urged that the commitments and emphases we have inherited from the last two or three hundred years of biblical studies and the last century of educational priorities generally work against reading the Bible in just this way—as Scripture. This is because they tend toward a concern with method over posture, and are possessed of an anemic view of learning. The practices of interpretation that have arisen since the late 1700s are not thereby cast aside, but they are dethroned.

Hermeneutics since Hans-Georg Gadamer has insisted that we bring with us always and everywhere our selves—our presuppositions and histories, our stories.[30] And these presuppositions enable

24

our understanding, as well as disable it. We cannot escape our histories because it is in them that our identity is generated. We cannot jump out of our skins. The miracle is that our horizons can be enlarged, our embodied lives transformed. As Scripture, the Bible is present as an alternative framework within which to construe our lives, and so challenges those who would be Christian by calling for a creative transformation of the patterns by which we make sense of our lives, and by which we interact with and within the world.

Chapter Two

Aims and Assumptions

N o weekend seminar on how to read the Bible will prepare persons for engaging the Bible as Scripture. There are no secrets that, once we are initiated into them, will effectively loosen God's voice or open our ears to hear God's address in our reading of the Bible. To take the Bible as Scripture is a theological statement and to attune our lives to receive it as Scripture is to adopt a theological stance. We locate ourselves on a particular map and within a particular community identified by its peculiar posture vis-à-vis these texts. It is first a matter of what we bring with us to the interpretive task, in terms of our allegiances and commitments, our taken-for-granteds, and not first in terms of which methodological toolbox we carry.

Reading the Scriptures at Pentecost

What aims and assumptions promote and guide our reading of the Bible as Scripture? Consider, for example, those gathered at

Pentecost. "Bewildered," or "puzzled," Luke describes them, "and astonished" (Acts 2:12). These are responses characteristic of those who witnessed the outpouring of the Spirit at Pentecost, and why not? These are extraordinary events, after all—extraordinary when taken on their own terms, but even more extraordinary when heard as Luke presents the story, full of echoes and reverberations from Israel's own history. The sound of winds raging; flame-like tongues, scores of them; an international, carnivalesque admixture of languages, some familiar and others belonging to an all-but-forgotten past—befuddlement and wonder may well be the anticipated responses to such phenomena as these. In fact, the entire passage, Acts 2:1-21, pivots around the question posed in verse 12, "What does this mean?"

Events do not generally come to us labeled, self-interpreting, so biblical faith requires and promotes a hermeneutical enterprise. As Luke makes clear in this text, essential to the work of faithful interpretation is a people formed by the Scriptures, Israel's own story, and minds "opened" by the Holy Spirit. The events of this day are quickly recited; the rest of Luke's narrative is given over to the work of scriptural interpretation.

First, the gift of the Spirit, together with its effects, demonstrates the central importance of what we might call charismatic hermeneutics. Tongue-speaking leads to the indictment, "They are filled with new wine" (v. 13), but we should not imagine that this is because Jesus' followers are speaking gibberish or otherwise behaving out of sorts. To those with the appropriate language repertoire, Pentecostal speech makes perfect sense: "*in our own languages* we hear them speaking about God's deeds of power" (v. 11). Moreover, the rare word Luke uses of their inspired utterance, *apophthengomai* (v. 4), is also found in Acts in 2:14, where it points to Peter's prophetic interpretation of Scripture; and 26:25, where it is explicitly contrasted with "raving" or "being out of one's mind" (*mainomai*). Their speech—intelligible and also inspired and doxological—is taken up with relating the mighty acts of God in Israel's history, "God's deeds of power" (see Pss. 106:2; 145:4, 12; Exod. 15).

More explicit are the ways Luke ties the Pentecostal outpouring of the Spirit into Israel's history and hope. Israel's Scriptures give meaning to Pentecost at the same time that Pentecost shows how to embody the scriptural story. Among these links to the Scriptures, the most direct comes in Peter's interpretive citation of Joel 2:28-32. Before this, however, we are driven back even further into the story, back to God's purpose in creation.

The ancient will of God is sounded in important allusions to the story of Babel in Acts 2. In spite of periodic suggestions by scholars, we find no "reversal of Babel" in Luke's story and, indeed, we would be mistaken to imagine that Babel needed reversing in the first place. Genesis 11 does not present the confusion of languages on the plain of Shinar simply as a punitive action on God's part. Instead, God's purpose from the beginning was for the human family to scatter across and fill the whole earth, and this is what God accomplishes at Babel (see Gen. 1:28; 9:1; 10:32; 11:8). Pushing further, what has frustrated God's purpose in Genesis 11 is not merely the collusion of humanity against God's purpose. Rather, the wickedness of this idolatrous plan is betrayed in the opening of the Babel story, with its reference to "one language"—a metaphor in the ancient Near East for the subjugation and assimilation of conquered peoples by a dominant nation.[1] Linguistic domination is a potent weapon in the imperial arsenal, as people of Luke's world themselves would have known, living as they did in the wake of the conquest of "the world" by Alexander the Great and the subsequent creation of a single, Greek-speaking linguistic community. God's scattering the people at Babel was already an act of grace, therefore, and, in an ironic way, God's intervening in Genesis 11 to thwart humanity's common building project actually opens up again fresh possibilities for human community. This is what comes to expression in Pentecost.

If God deconstructs a coerced unity in Genesis 11,[2] Acts provides no invitation to return to a single language as a divine blessing or gift. Pentecost is not a call to gather in a single place, the center of the earth, but the place of launching for a missionary movement to "the end of the earth" (1:8, my translation). What are we to make of the language miracle? When reading Acts 2, we must remember that, for this missionary activity to commence, speaking in the old, native languages of those gathered was simply unnecessary. Had those disciples merely spoken in Greek, all would have understood; Alexander's march across the Mediterranean world guaranteed that. Rather, like Babel, Pentecost is about the divine enabling of languages, but a key difference is signaled in the midst of similarity. Acts 2 begins and ends with Luke's report of the unity of human community (vv. 1, 42-47), but this koinonia is not the consequence of political domination, and unity is not instituted at the expense of distinctions among human communities. With the outpouring of the Spirit, koinonia is realized, not as the consequence of a single, repressive language, nor by the dissolution of multiple languages, nor by the disintegration of social and regional distinctives in the formation of cultural homogeneity. Rather, koinonia results from the generative activity of the Spirit who is poured out by Jesus (v. 33) and the location of a new rallying point of identity among those "who [call] on the name of the Lord" and baptized "in the name of Jesus Christ" (vv. 21, 38).

Luke locates the outpouring of the Spirit in relation to other points in Israel's past, too, especially the tradition of Pentecost, a harvest festival celebrating God's provision and offering thanksgiving for God's good gifts. Operating even more in the foreground to bathe the Pentecostal events in meaning is Peter's citation of the prophet Joel in Acts 2:17-21.

The prophet Joel is quoted as a "hermeneutical aside," interpreting these events in pictures borrowed from the Scriptures. It is worth remembering, then, that Jesus has already "opened" Peter's mind to understand the Scriptures (Luke 24:45) and poured the Spirit on Peter so that he might expound them faithfully. Peter is empowered to discern the affinity of the Joel text to his own community. He is a Spirit-inspired interpreter of Scripture. As such, his citation of the biblical text is not word for word, but already interpretive. Four motifs are central:

- Joel is tasked with providing a timetable within which to make sense of recent events (from the crucifixion through the outpouring of the Spirit) and the mission set in motion by the reception of the Spirit. These are "the last days" (v. 17), even if the "the Lord's great and glorious day" (v. 20) remains a future expectation.

• Premium is given to prophecy and divine revelation. In continuity with Israel's history, this suggests that followers of Jesus comprise a community of prophets who access the counsel of God and serve a destabilizing role in the larger world on account of their unrelenting faithfulness to God and their questioning rather than validating those habits of national and religious life that compete with God's counsel.

• Peter emphasizes the universal mission and promise of salvation. The terms are emphatic, allowing for no restrictions whatsoever, apart from response to the call to discipleship itself: "all flesh," "everyone who calls on the name of the Lord." This salvation, as Luke will show, is tied up with the restoration of God's people through forgiveness, the reception of the Spirit, and incorporation into the community of God's people through hospitality and baptism.

• Finally, if calling "upon the name of the Lord" bears this weighty significance, it is crucial to identify correctly who is this Lord. For readers of Joel, the answer is obvious: Yahweh. For the larger Roman world, the answer is equally transparent: the giver of divine blessings. For Acts, these two answers coalesce in Jesus, who, through his exaltation, has been installed as God's coregent, who shares in God's identity, and through whom divine beneficence is available (2:29-36).

Generated by the Pentecostal Spirit, the church now embodies and broadcasts the interpreted Scriptures. Their minds having been opened by the risen Lord to understand the Scriptures, and now, recipients of the Pentecostal Spirit, the disciples are empowered by the Spirit both to fathom the significance of the dramatic events that have transpired at this feast and to communicate their significance in ways that draw those events into the ancient purpose of God. They weave together Pentecostal phenomena, the story of Jesus, and the witness of Israel's Scriptures. The result is a community generated by the Spirit, shaped by the proclaimed Word.

What aims and assumptions guide our engagement with the Bible as Scripture? What patterns of faith and thought operate at a precognitive level, setting the compass for our interpretive work? This example of biblical interpretation brings several to the forefront, not the least of which is the immediacy of the Scriptures—that is, their capacity to speak clearly not only to their first audiences but also to later peoples faced with fresh challenges. In fact, this "immediacy" or "simultaneity" of God's voice in the Bible opens our view to a constellation of aims and assumptions that might guide our reading of the Bible as Scripture. Among the possibilities that might be developed, I want to mention three: the status of the Old Testament as Christian Scripture; the relation of Scripture to conversion or transformation; and the question, What might it mean for us to read these documents as though they were addressed to us? I will turn to the related concerns of the unity of Scripture and its authority in chapter 5.

The Old Testament as Christian Scripture

What I have in mind is the status and role of the Old Testament within the two-testament, Christian canon—an issue that surfaced prominently in the nineteenth century in the theology of Friedrich Schleiermacher, which has subsequently become even more pressing under the hegemony of the historical-critical paradigm in scholarship of the Hebrew Bible, and that is displayed week after week in the virtual absence of the Old Testament from the church. For many Christians, to our detriment, the Old Testament has been practically decanonized. That we must address the question of the Old Testament is an embarrassment to the church, rooted deeply in our history and on display among many of our theologians and in many of our pulpits.

With regard to Schleiermacher, we should note particularly the explicit statement regarding the relation of theology and the Bible that appears at the head of his discussion "The Formation of the Dogmatic System": "*All propositions which claim a place in an epitome of Evangelical (Protestant) doctrine must approve themselves both by appeal to Evangelical confessional documents, or in default of these, to the New Testament Scriptures, and by exhibition of their homogeneity with other propositions already recognized.*"[3] The importance of this statement is underscored when we recall Schleiermacher's legacy as the "father of Protestant theology"; reading him now one hundred seventy-five years later, we may be astonished by the staying power of his approach.

Schleiermacher's use of "New Testament" to modify "Scriptures" makes explicit what has been and continues often to be the practice associated with the church in its diminishing or completely negating the status and role of the Old Testament as Christian Scripture. In this, Schleiermacher was heir to the agenda established in the dawning years of modern historical criticism, under Johann Philipp Gabler, whose biblical-theological method emphasized the paradigmatic role of the New Testament. Schleiermacher also bears witness to what is almost certainly the inevitable outcome of the impulses of history-oriented analysis. Requiring that the meaning of texts resides at their historical address, historical criticism has no intrinsic need and little room for the theological claim constituted by the joining together of these two collections as one "book." Of course, it could be argued, and rightly so, that the Hebrew Scriptures *needed* to be rescued from New Testament dominion in Christian practices of interpretation. The Old Testament needed to be heard in terms of its own witness rather than employed as an arsenal of typological proof texts that blatantly turned Old Testament figures and data into precursors of Christ and the church.

More pointedly, Schleiermacher saw his disjunction of Old and New Testaments as the disjunction of Judaism and Christianity. Admitting the historical connection between Christianity and Judaism "through the fact that Jesus was born among the Jewish people" (§12.1), he nonetheless lumped Judaism together with heathenism "inasmuch as the transition from either of these to Christianity is a transition to another religion" (§12.2). He continues, "Christianity cannot in any wise be regarded as a remodeling or a renewal and continuation of Judaism" (§12.2). This does not mean that the widespread view that the church has displaced Israel as God's chosen, a doctrine known as supersessionism, necessarily requires antipathy toward the Old Testament. In fact, traditional supersessionism needs the Old Testament in order both to demonstrate the failure of Israel (and hence the need for a replacement people) and to anticipate Christ and the church. Even this tradition marginalizes the Old Testament, however, treating it as a kind of historical prefix to the advent of Christ or relegating it to the status of prophecy in need of fulfillment, rather than as divine revelation in its own right.[4]

From the standpoint of reading the New Testament, the disestablishment of the place of the Old Testament in the two-testament Christian canon prompts a theological crisis often overlooked, for one of its practical effects is its identification of the Old Testament as simply one of several possible presuppositions for reading the New Testament. It is "background," with the approximate status of other ancient Jewish books, such as 1 Enoch or the Testaments of the Twelve Patriarchs; non-Jewish texts, such as the Epic of Gilgamesh; or the texts and artifacts of Greek and Roman religion. This is problematic *historically*, since it fails to account for the role of Israel's Scriptures in the formation of Christian self-understanding, and *theologically*, since it makes optional the theological inheritance into which the New Testament is inscribed.[5]

In Christopher Seitz's study of the enduring theological witness of the Old Testament, we find a much-needed corrective. For him it is important to maintain that "the OT's per se voice functions normatively for Christian theological construction."[6] The Old Testament demands to be heard *as Christian Scripture*, apart from its appropriation in the New Testament, and this for theological reasons. Because God has spoken and acted in the Old Testament and because the New Testament affirms and does not challenge this basic theological claim, the Christian is obliged to hear the Old Testament as a discrete witness irrespective of how New Testament writers might have understood it. To claim the Old Testament as Christian Scripture in this sense is therefore to recognize that the voice we hear in the Old Testament is neither non- nor pre-Christian. For Seitz, then, what holds the canon together is not some sort of Scripture principle or theological abstraction, but the God who liberated Israel from slavery and raised Jesus from the dead. Christians who, for whatever reason, whether explicitly or functionally, downplay or deny the ongoing theological witness of the Old Testament thus cut themselves off from more than interesting or important "background material." At stake, rather, is the fullness of God's self-disclosure—that is, the possibility that we might erroneously imagine that we have access to a "'person-event Jesus of Nazareth' apart from the claims of the triune God."[7]

By way of example, consider the theological hermeneutic we find in 1 Peter 1:10-12:

> Concerning this salvation the prophets, who prophesied concerning the grace that has come to you, searched and explored, inquiring into what person or what sort of time was meant when the Spirit of Christ that was in them was testifying in advance to the sufferings coming to Christ and his subsequent glories. It was revealed to them that they were not serving themselves but you in these matters— matters that have now been announced to you through those who

evangelized you through the Holy Spirit sent from heaven, matters on which angels yearn to gaze. (my translation)

As is often noticed, here is a "hermeneutical key"[8] or, better, a theological hermeneutic of what we now call the Old Testament, with
Peter intimating how the Old Testament Scriptures must be read: as
"testifying in advance to the sufferings coming to Christ and his subsequent glories," and in continuity with the faithful community of
God's people, a continuity made possible by the Holy Spirit. Here is
a theological pattern by which to order the prophetic witness. What
is problematic is the suggestion that this theological pattern is the
consequence of reading with a new lens provided by the advent of
Christ.[9] What Peter makes clear, actually, is that this theological
pattern is resident already in the Scriptures of Israel themselves.
The issue is not that we are taught by the advent of Christ to read
the Scriptures retrospectively, but that the Christ in whom
Christians place their trust and now worship is the same Christ who
long ago revealed the ways of God in the Scriptures. The Venerable
Bede, commenting on 1 Peter 1:12 early in the eighth century, put
it this way:

> He had said previously that the spirit of Christ had foretold his
> sufferings and subsequent glories to the prophets, and now he says
> that the apostles are proclaiming the same things to them by the
> Holy Spirit sent from heaven. Hence it is evident that the same
> spirit of Christ was formerly in the prophets as was afterwards in
> the apostles, and therefore each was preaching the same faith in
> the suffering and subsequent glory of Christ to the peoples, the
> [prophets] that it was still to come, the [apostles] that it had
> already come; and because of this [they preached] that there is
> one Church, part of which preceded the bodily coming of the
> Lord, part of which followed [it].[10]

Interpretively, then, Israel's Scriptures testify to the Christ (and none other) who first inspired them.

How does this hermeneutic work itself out in 1 Peter? An important example is found in Peter's claim in 2:21-25 that Christ actualizes the role of the Servant of the Lord in Isaiah 52:13–53:12. At one level, we can allow that the suffering of Christ serves Peter as a theological assumption from which to read the Scriptures and make sense of them for Christians in the world. However, this is not because Isaiah 53 waited for the advent of Christ in order to be understood in relation to Christ. Nor is it merely that Peter found in Isaiah 53 a "prophecy" awaiting its "fulfillment" in Christ. Instead, the suffering of Christ and the suffering of Yahweh's Servant point to the same reality in God's purpose: God's saving purpose on behalf of a sinful people accomplished in the suffering of Yahweh's righteous servant. Inspired by the Spirit of Christ, Isaiah's text testifies to the saving economy of God, so that the proper context within which to read Isaiah 53 is conceptualized theologically as the terrain in which God actualizes his purpose. From this perspective, we would do violence to the text were we to treat it merely as a literary artifact or historical curiosity, or press it into the service of an agenda other than the outworking of God's aims.[11]

The hermeneutical issue that must be resolved in Christian appropriation of the Old Testament resides in the abundance of possible readings of Israel's Scriptures, its surplus of meaning. We cannot escape the multiple expressions of Israel's heritage in the first century, presumably any of which could demonstrate from the Scriptures that their community and its members comprised the heirs of Israel. Are we left to the conclusion, to each community its own valid reading? How might we differentiate among them? How might we know when or that the Scriptures are read aright (i.e., within the context of the divine economy)? Peter's theological hermeneutic rests in a mode of understanding that takes seriously how theological commitments shape or order our reading of Scripture. In this case, the suffering-and-vindicated Christ and the Scriptures of Israel are mutually informing, with the Scriptures demonstrating how to read Christ and Christ demonstrating which reading of Scripture has divine sanction. Faithful readings of the Old Testament take seriously its witness "in advance to the sufferings coming to Christ and his subsequent glories" and lead to communities of the faithful people of God. Why should we trust that such readings are divinely sanctioned? We do so not because Peter does historical analysis better than the Pharisees do, nor because Peter follows the literary structure of the passages in question better than do the Qumran sectarians (as important as these interpretive procedures might be). Instead, we do so because Peter actualizes the Scriptures in a way that coheres with their generation long ago, a coherence guaranteed by the Spirit of Christ.

Again, this does not mean that the words of the prophets were devoid of revelatory value before Christ; after all, God made known to the prophets that their words were anticipatory (v. 12). It does mean, though, that the prophets lacked the patterns of thinking and believing necessary to grasp fully the significance of what was before them. (In this regard, they are not much different from Jesus' disciples, as I am about to demonstrate, or from we who read the words of the Bible but do not hear in them the voice of God.) Even more so, it means that Peter finds an essential unity in the outworking of God's purpose, from the Scriptures of Israel to the community of Christ's followers—a unity that coheres in the one God, Yahweh, who raised Jesus from the dead; and in the Holy Spirit, who inspired the prophets of old and the evangelists who proclaimed the message of the prophets as good news.

Hence, a "Christian" reading of the Old Testament has no need to assert the superiority of the New Testament over the Old, nor that the Old Testament requires the New as its hermeneutical key. Rather, Christians recognize that the Old Testament points beyond itself toward the fulfillment of God's purpose at the same time that it narrates the expression of that purpose in creation and among those whom God has made his people. To interpret the pages of the biblical texts in this way is itself already a theological task that presumes an openness to a living relationship with God, on the basis of which we come to Scripture with respect, in gratitude, and ready to embrace and to be embraced into God's own ways and work.

> **The Old Testament points beyond itself toward the fulfillment of God's purpose at the same time that it narrates the expression of that purpose in creation and among those whom God has made his people.**

Scripture and "Conversion"

The activation of the converted mind is both an assumption of reading the Bible as Scripture and the goal of such a reading. I will develop this claim by returning to the narrative of Luke-Acts, one of the most puzzling features of which is the obtuseness of the disciples when it comes to understanding Jesus' work within the purpose of God. This obtuseness comes into focus above all in two parallel texts:

> "Let these words sink into your ears: The Son of Man is going to be betrayed into human hands." But they did not understand this saying; its meaning was concealed from them, so that they could not perceive it. And they were afraid to ask him about this saying. (Luke 9:44-45)

> Then he took the twelve aside and said to them, "See, we are going up to Jerusalem, and everything that is written about the Son of Man by the prophets will be accomplished. For he will be handed over to the Gentiles; and he will be mocked and insulted and spat upon. After they have flogged him, they will kill him, and on the third day he will rise again." But they understood nothing about all these things; in fact, what he said was hidden from them, and they did not grasp what was said. (Luke 18:31-34)

What is puzzling, even distressing, is that we find in the Gospel of Luke not one but two such reports. We might not be surprised by the first, located as it is at the end of the Galilean section of the Gospel of Luke but before the long journey that will occupy Jesus and his disciples from Luke 9 to 19. It is in the journey that Jesus engages especially in disciple formation; this section comprises instruction for the most part, and this teaching is mostly aimed at the disciples. Having begun in such a disappointing way (9:44-45), surely, as the journey draws to its close, the disciples will comprehend Jesus' words and the significance of his mission in the overarching purpose of God. Luke 18:31-34 is adamant on this point, however: "they did not grasp what was said."

Why are the disciples so slow to comprehend? One might suppose that God has concealed the meaning of Jesus' words from them.[12] However, in the context of revelatory prayer, "Turning to the disciples, Jesus said to them privately, 'Blessed are the eyes that see what you see!'" (10:23), and the disciples are those to whom the secrets of the kingdom are revealed (8:10); moreover, Jesus' injunction in 9:44 ("Let these words sink into your ears") presumes that they should be able to understand. Nevertheless, Luke's wording in 9:45 is emphatic: they lacked understanding; the meaning was hidden; they lacked perception; and they avoided discussing it further on account of their fear. What is more, their failure continues through the entire Gospel of Luke, until the concluding moments of Luke's narrative, when the impasse is broken, with Luke reporting that Jesus "opened their minds to understand the scriptures" (24:45). Prior to this, what is lacking are the categories of thought, an imagination adequate to correlate what Jesus holds together in his passion predictions, Jesus' exalted status and his impending dishonor.[13] They are unable to integrate in a seamless way how Jesus' messiahship could be defined with respect to both his elevated status before God and his rejection by human beings. Their patterns of thought and faith are too narrowly circumscribed, ordered as they are according to a conceptual scheme more conventional in Roman Palestine. Theirs are ill-formed imaginations, leading them to mouth the words, "What can this mean?"

The disciples' hermeneutical quandary finds its resolution in three related actions, noted in Luke 24 and Acts 1–2. First, the disciples have Jesus himself as their teacher, "opening the scriptures" to them (Luke 24:32). Second, Jesus "opened their minds to understand the scriptures" (24:45). Third, they are the recipients of the Holy Spirit, who enables inspired interpretation of the Scriptures (Acts 2).

How Jesus "opened the scriptures" is not immediately obvious from the Lukan narrative, which relates only that it was "necessary that the Messiah should suffer these things and then enter into his glory," and that "beginning with Moses and all the prophets, he interpreted to them the things about himself in all the scriptures" (24:25-27). Which Scriptures? We are not told; in fact, within the Lukan narrative, we have heard that the prophets or the Son of Man (and not the Messiah) "must suffer." Here, though, is where we find Jesus' hermeneutical lesson. By correlating the persecution of the prophets with messiahship, he is able to assert that the Scriptures provide a script for the eschatological king who would suffer before entering into glory.[14] Thus, in God's economy, the high status of God's anointed one is not contradicted by humility or humiliation. Instead, in his passion and exaltation, Jesus embodied the status reversal comprising salvation; his death was the focal point of the divine-human struggle over how life is to be lived, whether in humility or in self-elevation. Though righteous before God, though anointed by God, he is put to death. Rejected by people, he is raised up and vindicated by God—and all of this is subsumed under the one divine purpose. God's purpose embraces both rejection by humans and divine exaltation, and recognition of this fabula (that is, this story behind the story)—embraced so deliberately, embodied so fully by Jesus, the charismatic, authorized hermeneut—serves as the theological pattern by which to order the scriptural witness. The career of Jesus and the Scriptures of Israel thus bear witness to the same divine reality.

We can verify some of our thinking so far by inquiring, Who engages the Scriptures aright in the Gospel of Luke? There is the example of Jesus, of course, explicit in such texts as Luke 2:42-52; 4:1-13. There is Luke the narrator himself, but he does not speak directly regarding his interpretive habits. Other exemplars are Mary, Simeon, Zechariah, and Hannah, all within the Lukan birth narrative. Each interprets God's restorative work by deploying scriptural language and images by way of disclosing the significance of the advent of Jesus. Like Jesus, Simeon and Zechariah engage in interpreting Scripture as persons on whom the Spirit rests, who are filled with the Spirit. Luke has characterized each as responsive to God's salvific work in the world. And each engage in this reading of the Scriptures by way of setting out the nature of God's people, their identity and vocation.

The ensuing narrative of Acts is an extensive exercise in hermeneutics, in world shaping. Who grasps the significance of the outpouring of the Spirit at Pentecost? Who reads the Scriptures in conformity with the will of God? Importantly, in Acts, a vexing obstacle that must be overcome as God restores his people and both Jews and Gentiles are called to transfer their allegiances over to him is "ignorance."[15] This reality was observed by J.-W. Taeger, who saw that the human situation in Lukan thought was one characterized by ignorance. The problem for Taeger is that his analysis suffered from an anemic understanding of "knowledge" and "ignorance."[16] "Ignorance," for Luke, is less the state of "lacking information," and more "possessing a faulty view of God's reality." In other words, ignorance for Luke is actually misunderstanding—a failure at the most profound level to grasp adequately the purpose of God. Even when obeying God, people within the Lukan narrative obey him as they have come to perceive him, and the extent of their misperception is so grand that their attempts at obedience actually run counter to the divine will. That is, so long as they were committed to their former way of construing the nature of God and life before God, they were blinded to what God was doing. What is needed is a theological transformation: a deep-seated conversion in their conception of God and, thus, in their commitments, attitudes, and everyday practices. Consequently, the resolution of "ignorance" is not simply "the amassing of facts," but a realignment with God's ancient purpose, now coming to fruition (in other words, "conversion") and divine forgiveness. Luke's work is thus a narrative of enlightenment so that prior understandings might be razed and the now-reconstructed understanding of the purpose and promises of God, an understanding that arises from the story of the Scriptures as Luke narrates it, might be welcomed.

According to Peter's address at Pentecost, the exaltation of Jesus and the consequent outpouring of the Holy Spirit have signaled a dramatic transformation in history, so the message of Jesus' witnesses calls for a radically different understanding of the world than that held previously. Within the speeches of Acts, Jewish people might hear the familiar stories borrowed from their Scriptures, but these stories have been cast in ways that advocate a reading of that history that underscores the fundamental continuity between the ancient story of Israel, the story of Jesus, and the story of the Way. Israel's past (and present) is understood accurately and embraced fully only in relation to the redemptive purpose of God, and this divine purpose comes to decisive expression in Jesus' ministry, crucifixion, and exaltation, and through exegetes operating in the sphere of the Holy Spirit. The coming of Jesus as Savior may signal the fresh offer of repentance and forgiveness of sins to Israel (Acts 5:31; 13:38-39), but the acceptance of this offer by Jewish people is dependent on their embracing *this interpretation* of God's salvific activity. Greek audiences, too, are asked to adopt a new way of viewing the world. Note how, at Athens, Paul distinguishes between how God worked in the past (17:30a; cf. 14:16) and how he will now operate (17:30b)—a distinction that is marked by Jesus' resurrection and that calls for conversion. And what is conversion, but transformation of the theological imagination, which includes incorporation into the community of believers and concomitant practices?[17]

In short, as the Lukan narrative urges, Scripture and Christian conversion become inseparably interwoven. His perspective is not grounded in a particular technique or pattern of conversion.[18] Nor is it that Luke emphasizes the transformative effects of the moment of conversion. Instead, conversion as Luke develops it entails a reconstruction of one's self within a new web of relationships, a transfer of allegiances, and the embodiment of transformed dispositions and attitudes.[19] For both Jew and Gentile, conversion is the transference of allegiances that govern one's life; in the case of the Jew, this has to do especially with reformed conceptions of God's character and purpose, whereas for the Gentile it has to do with trusting the one true God, the living God. In either case, this is the God whose character and design are known through Jesus Christ. Luke thus presents the Scriptures as a narrative of enlightenment: razing prior patterns of thinking, acting, feeling, and faith, and constructing in their stead an understanding of the purpose and promises of God comprehended by means of the life, death, and resurrection of Jesus.

For Luke, this means that conversion is deeply embedded in the ancient story of God's dealings with Israel; it is to this God, the God of Israel known in and through the Scriptures, that life must be directed. Second, it means that this conversion is to a particular reading of that ancient story—a reading that insists that the only genuine line tracing the actualization of God's purpose passes through the life, death, and exaltation of Jesus, Messiah and Lord. Third, it means that this conversion is eschatologically driven, since it is the eschatological outpouring of the Spirit that marks the turn of the ages, that motivates the Christian call to conversion, and that makes conversion possible. One of Luke's primary contributions to our understanding of the concept and experience of conversion, then, is this emphasis on the grand narrative of God's ancient and ongoing purpose.

How does this take place? Conversion entails *autobiographical reconstruction*. As Peter Berger and Thomas Luckmann put it, "Everything preceding the alternation is now apprehended as leading toward it . . . everything following it as flowing from its new reality. This involves a reinterpretation of past biography *in toto*, following the formula 'Then I *thought* . . . now I *know*.'"[20] Conversion shatters one's past and reassembles it in accordance with the new life of the converted. Additionally, conversion is the process of *embracing new patterns of thinking, feeling, believing, and acting*—a process that centers on grasping the purposes of God and being written into the history of God's engagement with Israel. Converts find explanations for phenomena in terms that are appropriate to the new structure of beliefs they have embraced and that are often distinctive from the belief structures held by others; in our case, the whole of Israel's history and self-understanding is now reevaluated for presentation in light of the newly found understanding of God's purpose resident in Jesus' crucifixion and exaltation.

Conversion, then, is the transference of one's orienting commitments, which gives rise to and is confirmed in community-nested practices appropriate to those new allegiances and which opens the way to ongoing transformation as one comes more fully to embrace and indwell this new life-world. Conversion is reorientation, a "changing of the world," which shatters one's past and reassembles it in accordance with the new life of the community of the converted. Life is apprehended within a new structure of meaning, as one is enabled to reconceptualize the character of the people of God as this is plotted in Scripture, and is manifest in the community of God's people who are constituted by this biblical narrative, and whose practices embody this spirituality and leverage the ongoing conversion of its membership.

For characters within the Lukan narrative, conversion is the consequence of this rendering of the story of God and his purpose, a reconception of the biblical drama. For those of us engaged with Luke's narrative as Christian Scripture, conversion is the consequence of embracing this story as our own, and seeing the plotline of our lives as continuous with and an ongoing extension of the narrative that, for Luke, begins with the promise to Abraham, celebrates New Exodus in the advent of Christ, continues on in the expansion of the mission to all people, and leans forward into the eschaton. Both of us—God's people then and God's people now—are the church constituted by the Scriptures read in this way, a people who stand under these Scriptures open to their formative influence and direction.

Whose Mail?

To whom are the biblical materials addressed? At first, the answer seems obvious—obvious, at least, in the case of many books of the New Testament. Paul's Letter to the Romans is manifestly written to Christians in Rome, the Corinthian letters to those in Corinth, and Revelation to the seven churches enumerated in Revelation 2–3. Though the addressees are not often labeled so explicitly, books in the genre "Old Testament Introduction" or "New Testament Introduction" generally agree that pronouncements can be made for each book: when and why it was written, by whom, for whom, and the like. One of the staples of biblical studies has been the initial need to tie a document to its original context, the moment of its generation. Micah addressed those people in those circumstances. Jude addressed others in other circumstances. The twenty-first-century reader in the United States, then, is cast in the unenviable position of reading someone else's mail. For the historian, this is enough, since the aim of reading is to gain insight into the past. The historian can even demonstrate an interest in the theology of these texts from another time, since the message of those texts is subject to description and analysis in the service of questions such as, What did Obadiah or James intend to teach their target audiences?

So pervasive is this way of thinking that it is now difficult to imagine any other possibilities. "Meaning" belongs to the past. "Meaning" refers to what the original author intended to communicate. How could it be otherwise? Yet, for a reading of the Bible as Scripture, another way must be found. This is because, in the same way that to refer to the Bible as Scripture is a theological statement, to speak of the church, theologically, is to speak of its oneness across time and space. There is only one people of God.

That is, *historical* judgments about the audience of a biblical text stand in tension with the *theological* affirmation of the oneness of the church that receives this biblical text *as Scripture*. Historical criticism assumes what Christians can never assume, namely, that there is more than one people of God. The eminent Lutheran theologian Robert Jenson has observed, "*The initiating error of standard modern exegesis is that it presumes a sectarian ecclesiology*"—one that fails to acknowledge that "the text we call the Bible was put together in the first place by the same community that now needs to interpret it."[21] Similarly, writing from a self-styled "baptist" theological perspective,

James McClendon offers an account of biblical authority that finds its center in this "hermeneutical motto": "*The present Christian community as the primitive community and the eschatological community.* In other words, the church now is the primitive church and the church on the day of judgment is the church now; the obedience and liberty of the followers of Jesus of Nazareth is *our* liberty, *our* obedience."[22] McClendon is quick to point out that this "motto" provides no impetus for dismissing the hard work of biblical scholarship. In fact, the opposite might be claimed. Taking seriously Scripture's ongoing theological relevance and authority presses even more the need for the work of interpretation. As early Jewish interpretation of Torah recognized, a commitment to these texts as Scripture requires extending their meaning from the past into the present, with "readers fighting to find what they must in the holy text."[23]

It may be worth noting that impulses in this direction reside already in biblical texts themselves. First Peter, for example, addresses groups of Christians across an expansive geography, but never differentiates among them. Peter seems to regard them as a single church or "household," sharing the same gospel, struggling with the same realities. Moreover, 1 Peter ties the situation of his audience to that of all believers: "The same kind of sufferings are being accomplished in the case of your family of believers throughout the world" (5:9, my translation). This has the effect of broadening the application and appeal of Peter's letter to the whole of the Christian family. Appeals of this kind are hardly unique in the New Testament. Beginning his letter, Paul may explicitly mention the Corinthians, it is true, but the apostle goes on to include "all those who in every place call on the name of our Lord Jesus Christ, both their Lord and ours" (1 Cor. 1:2; see 2 Cor. 1:1). And in a letter specifically addressed to "the saints . . . in Colossae" (Col. 1:2), we find this directive: "When this letter has been read among you, have it read also in the church of the Laodiceans; and see that you read also the letter from Laodicea" (Col. 4:16). Accordingly, the subsequent theological location of these documents within the Christian canon preserves and promulgates a momentum toward catholicity already present within them.

If Paul writes a letter to the Romans, then the "address" of his message is surely Rome. But if this letter is relocated in a collection of Pauline letters circulating throughout the empire, then the "address" of his message is expanded to the empire. And if this letter is further relocated in a collection of documents regarded as canonical, then the "address" of that message is expanded further, to account now for its significance within the canon. And if this canon is received as the church's Scriptures, then a further theological claim has been made: this letter is addressed to the church, and so to us. On this basis, we reiterate our earlier claim that the essential character of the division between the world of the Bible and our own is not *historical* but theological. It has to do with a theological vision, the effect of which is our willingness to regard these biblical texts as our Scripture and to inhabit its message—its world—as our own.

This transformation of address comes with a price. We might rather read Paul's Letter to the Romans as a letter from the apostle to our forebears in the faith who made their home in ancient Rome.

Doing so, we can reflect on their problems, and watch, sometimes with glee, sometimes in bewilderment, at how Paul addresses their circumstances. We can wonder what they might have done to merit that kind of admonition. We can achieve expertise in Paul's Letter to the Romans, map its argument, and codify its theological points. We can do all of this without ever having personally to hear or feel the challenge of the letter. After all, it was written to them, then.

Consider, instead, the Letter of James. This letter is addressed to "the twelve tribes in the Dispersion" (1:1), to whom James speaks repeatedly in the second person: "you." Who is the "you" to whom James addresses this letter? These are folk metaphorically identified with the Jews exiled from their homeland at the behest of Babylon. They are, then, "not at home." They are folk whose lives are lived on the margins of acceptable society, whose deepest allegiances and dispositions do not line up well with what matters most in the world in which they live. Indeed, along the way, James refers to "trials of any kind" (1:2), the "testing of your faith" (1:3), humiliation (1:9), "temptation" (1:12), "distress" (1:27), "conflicts and disputes" (4:1), victims of fraudulent behavior (5:4), condemnation and murder (5:6), and a life of "wandering" (5:20). This letter is addressed to persons in exile, whose lives turn on the social, political, and religious threat confronting a people challenged with the perennial possibility and danger of assimilation and defection. Simply put, they do not belong.

We may happily reconstruct our portrait of the recipients of the Letter of James in historical terms. We may be less happy to read it as though it were addressed to us—or, perhaps more accurately, to read ourselves into this letter as though it were addressed to us. After all, who among us wishes for our lives to be characterized in these ways? This is not the existence we have chosen for ourselves. We do not desire the status of societal misfits, deviants in the world around us. But if this is true, then it is also true that we are not in a position to hear well the Letter of James *as Christian Scripture*.

All of the linguistic skills we might develop, all of the insight into historical background we might accumulate—none of this will make up for the basic reality that, as a whole, we Americans do not want to think of ourselves as dwelling on the world's margins. We choose our clothes otherwise. We choose our classes otherwise. We choose our friends otherwise. We are the First World, not Second or Third. We are the West; others are the non-West. We do not easily adopt a way of life that guarantees our minority status in the world. We want to belong. And, therefore, we do not easily hear God's address to us in James.

The problem is not our lack of information about folk in the first century. The problem is theological. What separates us from the biblical text is not "the strange world of the Bible" as much as its unhandy, inconvenient claims on our lives. We are not ready to be exiles in the dispersion. If James addresses itself to those whose lives are radically marked by their membership in a community defined by its allegiance to Christ, whose lives thus stand in an ambiguous relationship to the mores and values of the world around them, and, accordingly, whose practices attract for them opposition from their neighbors, then it is read best by those who share its theological assumptions and who hear its opening words as an invitation to embody its world. The question is whether we are ready to be included in a community defined in these terms.

Critical exegesis today tends toward a hermeneutical theory that presumes that we must make pilgrimage into the world of the biblical text in order to ascertain its truths, then return to our world in order to transform those truths into contemporary thought and language forms. The exegetical vision I am sketching presumes that the idea of "pilgrimage" is thus wrongly applied. "Pilgrimage" is more appropriately a description of the character of our lives in this world, with our status as strangers in the world attributable to our making our home in the world of Scripture. In this hermeneutical scenario, it is not the message of the Bible that requires transformation; it is we who require transformation.

We can approach this issue of "audience" from another perspective. In a way derivative of the church's recognition of the status of James and other biblical materials as Scripture, I am also concerned with the recovery of the reader in recent interpretive theory and particularly the recognition of the church's status as a readerly community. Early in the twentieth century, innovations in hermeneutical theory began to shift the weight of emphasis from interpretation as the discovery of meaning contained within a text toward interpretation as the generation of meaning. Accordingly, emphasis is placed on the process whereby "the right of the reader and the right of the text converge in an important struggle that generates the whole dynamic of interpretation."[24] From this perspective, one's historical and cultural distance from the text erects no barrier to but is a necessary factor in the process of interpretation.

Persons weaned on historical criticism may rightly be anxious about my urging a reader-oriented approach to the letter's theology. After all, there are a range of readerly perspectives, and the results of some seem hardly at all to have much relation to the text alleged to have been read.[25] For this reason, I need to declare my interest in a particular kind of reader, the "Model Reader," as well as explain briefly what this means.

It is true that other readers might have impressed themselves into this task; in literary theory today we may have recourse to a surprising variety—implied readers, competent readers, authorial readers, informed readers, and real readers among them.[26] I find these other possibilities less helpful for reading the Bible as Scripture, however. For example, our access to Peter's *intended* readers or his *first flesh-and-blood* readers is limited by what we can project from the letter itself; hence, these categories falter for lack of firsthand descriptions or testimony. In any case, our concern with reading Scripture moves us beyond too narrow an interest in the voice or intent of the human author, in the direction of according privilege to the role of these texts in divine self-disclosure.

I have borrowed the concept of the Model Reader from Umberto Eco. He speaks of good reading as the practice of those who are able to deal with texts in the act of interpreting in the same way as the author dealt with them in the act of writing.[27] Such a reader is the precondition for actualizing the potential of a text to engage and transform us, for it is this reader whom the text not only presupposes but also nurtures. This requires that readers enter cooperatively into the discursive dance with the text while leaving open the possibility that the text may be hospitable to other interpretations.

Obviously, this approach eschews an interpretive agenda governed by readerly neutrality, that holy grail of biblical studies in the modern period. Equally obvious, it promotes a concern with the formation of persons and communities who embody and put into play, who perform, Scripture.

My use of the category of Model Reader does not allow apathy concerning historical questions, but recognizes that biblical texts are themselves present to us as cultural products, which, then, draw on, actualize, propagate, and/or undermine the context within which they were generated. In the case of Scripture, the notion of a Model Reader also recognizes the contextual location of biblical texts in larger, concentric circles. These include the complex network of intertextual connections that draw later biblical books into earlier ones and thereby extend their ongoing influence, canonical relations that enrich the possibilities of interpretive interplay at the same time that they bar readings that fall outside the parameters of the church's "rule," the story of the church's interpretation and embodiment of its Scriptures, as well as other ways of conceiving the ecclesial location of the Scriptures. This includes the contextualization of Scripture in relation to the church's practices of mission and song, baptism and eucharist, hospitality and prayer, service and proclamation, gathering and scattering.

This perspective is not unlike the kind of interpretive work championed by Karl Barth and examined by Richard Burnett.[28] Barth, however, helpfully, presses the notion of context even further. Scripture is foremost witness to the Word rather than source or repository of content, whether historical or cultural or theological.

The Word creates its hearer, who, then, is invited to participate in its subject, which is God. Interpreters are invited to think with the Scriptures, not about them. Context is pivotal, and historical context ought not be overlooked, but for Barth this is comparatively insignificant. "The fact that 'the whole Bible authoritatively proclaims that God must be *all in all*' meant that God Himself, that revelation, was the actual context in which the Bible was to be understood."[29] The adjective *comparatively* is crucial. No stranger to hard-nosed exegesis, Barth could nonetheless recognize the theological immediacy of Paul's Letter to the Romans: "If we rightly understand ourselves, our problems are the problems of Paul; and if we be enlightened by the brightness of his answers, those answers must be ours."[30]

As Model Readers generated by this text, we are guarded from too easily colonizing or objectifying the text, instead hearing its own voice from within its own various contextual horizons. At the same time, we remain open to the challenge of developing the habits of life that make us receptive to the vision of God, God's character and God's project, animating these texts as Scripture and, then, textualized in and emanating from these pages. We come to Scripture with dispositions of risky openness to a reordering of the world, repentance for attitudes of defiance of the grace of God's self-revelation, hospitable to a conversion of our own imagination.

Conclusion

We began by asking, What aims and assumptions promote and guide our reading of the Bible as Scripture? By way of addressing this question, I have engaged in conversation with some examples of interpretive work in the New Testament. From this, I have drawn attention above all to the immediacy (or simultaneity) of the Scriptures, that is, their capacity to speak clearly not only to their first audiences but also to later peoples faced with fresh challenges. In support of this emphasis I turned both to our theology of the church and to literary theory. Theologically, I have underscored an important ramification of the confession of the church as "one" and as "catholic": when, for example, Paul addressed his letter to the church at Rome, he was likewise addressing the church across time and geography. The Venerable Bede saw similarly in Peter's affirmations regarding the Spirit of Christ that "there is one Church, part of which preceded the bodily coming of the Lord, part of which followed [it]."[31]

These considerations entail, further, the status of the Old Testament as divine self-disclosure likewise addressed to God's people in all times and places. Old and New Testaments join in their singular witness to the God of Abraham and Sarah, the God who raised Jesus from the dead.

From the standpoint of literary theory, I have urged that we embrace the status of the Model Reader of these biblical texts. Were we to do so, we would not visit these ancient texts as though they were alien territory. We would not come to them as visitors at all, but rather would make our home in them even while recognizing that to do so would be to declare ourselves strangers in this world. We would take on the persona of their addressees, allowing the terms of these texts to address us: to critique, to encourage, to motivate, to

> **Scripture aims for its readers to embark on a journey of theological formation bounded only by the character and purpose of God.**

instruct, to redirect—that is, to shape us. For some persons, this might be attempted as an experiment; in the words of Ursula LeGuin quoted in the previous chapter: "The gesture need not be permanent, a lasting posture of the mind or heart; yet it is not false. It is more than the suspension of disbelief needed to watch a play, yet less than a conversion. It is a position, a posture in the dance."[32] At the same time, though, we recognize that what is "more than the suspension of disbelief . . . yet less than a conversion" is less than enough when it comes to the claims of the Bible as Scripture, to its aims. It aims for its readers to embark on a journey of theological formation bounded only by the character and purpose of God.

We have also seen in our engagement with these New Testament texts a certain circularity about the reading of Scripture. It is especially if not exclusively in them that we access God's disclosure, but they are capable of more than one reading. How do we sort among the readings? I will have more to say about criteria for validity in interpretation in chapter 4, so here want to make only one comment. Though in various ways, we find in New Testament texts the affirmation that the Scriptures are rightly read when they are read in relation to God's agenda in Christ. First Peter has it that it was the same Christ at work in the prophets and apostles bearing witness to the suffering and glory that marked Christ's own career. Similarly, Luke urges a reading of the Scriptures in relation to the fabula, or story behind the story, of how God gets things done—through the suffering and vindication of the righteous, decisively exemplified in Jesus of Nazareth. The circularity is this: we discern God's character and will in Scripture, but it is God's character and will that guide our reading of Scripture. How is this circularity to be resolved? We have already found hints of an answer in repeated references to the status of Christ as God's ultimate self-disclosure, to the work of the Spirit who inspires and guides scriptural interpretation, and to the ecclesial formation of persons as those whose interpretation of Scripture is not only an exercise in exegesis but, indeed, a home in which to dwell. These are the sorts of resources that will occupy us in the next chapter.

CHAPTER THREE

RESOURCES

R eading the Bible as Christian Scripture entails putting the theological disciplines back together. By "theological disciplines," I include the disciplines of theology and biblical studies, which despite perhaps good intentions and sometimes imaginative initiatives, have drifted apart,[1] but others besides. "Disciplines" refers not only to the theological curricula in a seminary or school of theology, but also to the habits of faith and life that occupy Christians more generally—to such practices of Christian formation as corporate worship, instruction, prayer, and hospitality. "Disciplines" refers as well to the ministries of God's people, whether structured or unstructured, characteristic of the church gathered or of the church scattered. Theological disciplines, understood with this variety, come to focus in reading the Bible as Scripture.

How best to model the relation of Scripture to the theological disciplines? More than two hundred years ago, Johann Philipp Gabler inspired what was to become the pervasive answer. He sketched a three-stage process by which one might move from biblical studies to theology: (1) linguistic and historical analysis of biblical texts, (2) identification of ideas common among the biblical writers, and (3) articulation of the Bible's timeless and universal principles.[2] This now widely shared proposal cultivated a hermeneutical commitment to observer neutrality with an unswerving focus on the historical rootedness of the text and the historical gap separating text and reader as key coordinates in the work of interpretation. The archetypal interpreter that emerged from this model is one who is not guided by theological commitments (or, indeed, by commitments of any kind, other than the bracketing of questions of "truth" in order to give priority to the question of "meaning"), with the result that the study of the biblical materials has long been denuded of inherent religious interests. Biblical scholars have increasingly regarded themselves as philologists and historians rather than theologians. At most, their job would be to describe the theological content or perspective of the biblical materials, leaving to others the constructive and prescriptive theological tasks.

In an address marking his inauguration as a professor of New Testament theology in a university context, Larry Hurtado inadvertently helps document the problem. First finding it necessary to affirm the essentially historical and critical nature of New Testament study, he goes on to add that "we cannot really study the New Testament writings without engaging the religious affirmations and issues that constitute their contents."[3] This is an important point that bears repeating in view of how often in the last three centuries history and theology have occupied opposite poles in biblical studies. At the same time, it is self-evident that study of the religious significance of these texts can itself be undertaken as a historical enterprise, unrelated to the potential voice of those texts in contemporary theological witness.

Removed from the hands of day-to-day Christians, biblical studies has come more and more to belong to professional biblical interpreters. Biblical scholars tend toward a view of themselves as those who alone understand "what was really going on" in the background of the text, and novices, even among the seminary trained, are generally happy to be told "what the Bible says"—since, it is obvious to all, the scholarly professional has the inside track on how to make sense of these ancient texts. With respect to reading the Bible as Scripture, I have urged, rather, that no amount of linguistic training or level of expertise in historical and textual analysis can supersede the more essential "preparation" entailed in such dispositions and postures as acceptance, devotion, attention, and trust. This does not mean that historical and textual analyses are immaterial, inappropriate, or unneeded. It does mean that these forms of critical analysis must take their place alongside other commitments rather than above them.

In this chapter, I will expand on these essential dispositions by exploring resources for our reading of the Bible as Christian Scripture. Recasting biblical studies as an inherently theological enterprise, I want to resist the common division of labor that identifies some (pastors, theologians) for their interest in speaking of God in the present tense while insisting that others (biblical scholars) confine themselves to speaking of God only in the past tense.

The predominant image would no longer be "building a bridge" from biblical scholarship to ecclesial community, or "crossing the bridge" from text to sermon, or journeying from exegesis to biblical theology to systematic theology to ethics. Instead, biblical studies would self-consciously locate itself *within* the church, just as the church works out its identity and mission for the sake of the world. Other ways of engaging the biblical materials might continue, of course. Theological engagement with Scripture has no need to exclude other interpretive agenda, but only insists that reading the Bible *as Scripture* has its own inherently theological presumptions, protocols, and resources. I will develop four of these, urging that our reading of the Bible as Scripture must be ecclesially located, theologically fashioned, critically engaged, and Spirit-imbued.

Reading Scripture Must Be Ecclesially Located

For those genuinely interested in the Bible as Scripture, the single most important practice to cultivate is involvement in interpreting Scripture with others who share this posture of "standing under," who meet regularly to discern its meaning for faith and life and put its message into play. The best interpreters are those actively engaged in communities of biblical interpretation. The biblical materials have their genesis and formation within the community of God's people. They speak most clearly and effectively from within and to communities of believers. No interpretive tool, no advanced training, can substitute for active participation in a community concerned with the reading and performance of Scripture. If such a group is multigenerational and multicultural, this is even better. Among the reasons for this, let me mention two.

First, the church engaging the Bible as Scripture is itself being shaped in the form of and by Scripture, and it serves both as crucial context within and the premier instrument by which God's people are formed as persons who embody Scripture. Remembering that the community of the people of God whose lives are on display in Scripture is none other than our community, we easily find ourselves in these texts, represented sometimes by those who embrace and sometimes those who resist the voice of God and the practices that help us better hear God's voice. Those who perform Scripture are themselves better outfitted to continue their performance and to apprentice others in this craft. By performance I do not mean playacting, of course. "Performance" assumes all of the seriousness of hearing, heeding, embodying, and giving expression to the character of God who makes himself known in Scripture. "Performance" might suggest an analogy with the musical or theatrical arts; either way, we find a script complete on its own, but that invites greater fulfillment, or activation, in the event of its performance. Performance speaks to creative fidelity: "fidelity" in the sense that the notes on the score or words in the playscript predetermine the parameters of

> **The church engaging the Bible as Scripture is itself being shaped in the form of and by Scripture.**

performance, "creative" in the sense that life is too particular and unruly to be carefully scripted, but Christians can nonetheless be persons shaped by this script as well as persons who understand the plotlines of life according to its lines and measures.[4]

My reference to a church *that engages the Bible as Christian Scripture* serves as an important precondition—one that, I fear, is not as easily or often met in contemporary expressions of the church as one might expect or hope. The strange silence of the Bible in the church is deafening, and, regularly, this is just as true for self-identified conservative as for self-styled liberal congregations; just as true for charismatic congregations as for those who shun all such labels. For often widely disparate reasons, the Scripture enjoys little play in churchly settings of all kinds—sometimes regarded as off-putting to seekers (or pre-Christians), for example, and sometimes regarded as irrelevant to the realities of the contemporary world.

Sometimes, though, the silence of the Bible in the church is masked by messages peppered with references to biblical texts and even to the central importance of the Bible. In these cases, the actual absence of any life-challenging or life-forming engagement with God's self-disclosure in Scripture is hidden behind those multiple references from or to the Bible that fill out slide presentations or sermon outlines. Though it was years ago, I remember my stunned reaction when, as a youth pastor, I discussed with the senior pastor the outline I had prepared as a college student for an address on a topic of contemporary interest. I possessed an exhaustive concordance, which I had put to good use in my efforts to support with biblical references each point I wanted to make. The senior pastor, himself no mean interpreter of biblical texts, remarked, simply, "I don't know how you are going to deal with all of those texts in a single presentation." *Deal with a text*—what did that mean?

That is, either as strangers to the "ugly ditch" separating the allegedly antiquarian interests of the biblical materials from life today, or as persons who have given up on the hard slogging apparently required to traverse the distance from the meaning of the Bible back then to its significance now, some pastors and teachers find themselves adopting more pragmatic uses of the Bible. In these scenarios, the Bible serves, for example, as a book of quotations from which to draw authoritative support for one's words, as a collection of proverbs for backing up moral convictions, or perhaps as a treasure chest of discussion starters for group interaction on day-to-day issues. Interest in this sort of application is often articulated in terms of a baseline assumption that the Bible is a resource book for life in this world—a kind of "owner's manual," indexed for troubleshooting when life goes wrong. In these churchly contexts, the words of the Bible may be visible, but it cannot be said that these are churches where the Bible is engaged as Christian Scripture. In such contexts, biblical accounts are formed into a collage of the teacher's making, with Bible verses plugged in where they seem best to fit. In such contexts, the considerable resources of the Bible are being shaped into messages for today, but the church is not itself being shaped in the form of Scripture. In such contexts, the church is shaping the Bible and not the Bible shaping the church. The gathering of Christ followers is neither that crucial context within nor that premier instrument by which God's people are formed as persons who embody Scripture.

However, perhaps just as often, responsibility for the muzzling of the Bible in the church lies in the opposite direction. If some fail to recognize the Bible as "other," others exaggerate the Bible's status as "other" into an insurmountable "distance." If for some the Bible is little more than the dummy sitting in the lap of the talented ventriloquist, for others the Bible has no voice at all. If some are inclined to read the Bible in an opportunistic way so as to relate this or that verse directly to a situation or need today, others find the challenges involved in interpreting biblical materials simply too complex and demanding for the would-be interpreter.

How can this be? Among several possible reasons, surely one of the primary ones is the ugly ditch that has opened up between biblical studies and the life of the church. The dilemma of the ugly ditch is the distance we have learned to imagine separating the world of the Bible from the world we inhabit, and, then, the sheer amount of work required of those who desire to render significant for life today a text whose meaning has by definition been relegated to antiquity.

Given my own location in the evangelical wing of the church, two brief illustrations may help demonstrate this last concern. As a visiting worshiper in a large international church, I had the opportunity to hear a person who may well be the premier evangelical statesman and expositor of the last half of the twentieth century. For forty-five minutes he took us, step by step, through the exegetical details of a text in 2 Corinthians 4, leading finally to the question, "Now, how shall we apply this text to today?" This led to a three-minute discussion of the importance of quiet time for Christian growth, an emphasis that, frankly, had more to do with the particular evangelical subculture of which he was a part than with the Pauline text. Second, while serving on the faculty of the American Baptist Seminary of the West, I shared the platform with a friend at a major conference on baptist identity, both of us tasked with leading those gathered in morning exercises in Bible study. My friend, a well-known evangelical New Testament scholar committed to a historical-critical paradigm of biblical interpretation, led us for two mornings in his reading of two difficult texts in Paul's Letter to the Romans. We were each allotted one hour each morning, and I could not help but observe that, on both occasions, my friend came to the end of the hour having never moved from "interpretation" to "application." Commenting on this before the audience, he observed, "I am sorry that we have run out of time before I was able to talk about the significance of this passage for us. But the historical background is so important!"

On these occasions, was the Bible presented as Christian Scripture? However one answers that question, it remains the case that, in both instances, clergy and lay alike might be forgiven for imagining that the work of biblical interpretation is so onerous, so demanding, that it should not, and probably could not, be done by mere mortals. Leave it to the professionals. The issues are too complex, the labyrinth leading from ancient meaning to contemporary application too challenging. Faced with an iron curtain of complications segregating ancient text and contemporary life, it may be little wonder that so many turn for inspiration to material other than the biblical writings, read on their own terms.

Reading the Bible as Christian Scripture, however, calls into question the whole notion that the church inhabits the contemporary world and so never really entertains the need for spanning the ugly ditch. This is not because the church flees from the contemporary world, but because it constitutes this world in terms of the world of Scripture and cultivates among its members the eyes and ears of faith to see and hear what is outside the sensory perception of those whose lives are not animated by faith. In the world disclosed by Scripture, the impossible and

> **In Scripture the impossible, unthinkable, and nonsensical are made possible, become the stuff of wisdom, and flood the senses.**

unthinkable and nonsensical are made possible, become the stuff of wisdom, and flood the senses. Who can forgive seventy times seven? How can the last be first? Who can make friends with the poor? Who can overcome without taking up arms? Only those who are already in the process of reimagining the world in terms set out by Scripture. Only those for whom reality is framed by Scripture, who see things as they really are because their patterns of thinking, feeling, believing, and behaving are being sculpted through their ongoing encounter with the whole of Scripture. Finding our home in its world, then, means opening ourselves within the church to the role of Scripture in shaping a people, transforming their most basic commitments, dispositions, and identities. We come to the text expecting it to tell us something. If the narrative of Scripture is a unitary story of the world we inhabit, then to be a Christian is to have our lives shaped in a decisive way by and taken up into this other larger story of God's redemptive agenda in the world.[5]

Second, the location of our work with the Bible as Scripture within the community of God's people serves as a pivotal interpretive constraint. The church protects the Bible, and us, from the myopia that would press us, however unwittingly, to substitute our word for God's.

Perhaps the most basic and enduring challenge of feminist hermeneutics in the closing decades of the twentieth century and subsequently is its recognition that all readings are "interested" and "located." This challenge is now one of the taken-for-granted coordinates for all sorts of exegetical endeavors—in the United States, including Latino/Latina and African American modes of interpretation, for example. Indeed, the disputation of objective, dispassionate readings of biblical texts is more and more a staple of critical biblical studies. As C. René Padilla urged in the early 1980s, interpretive approaches that set their compass by a supposed scientific objectivity are neither possible nor desirable.

> It is not possible, because contemporary interpreters are stamped with the imprint of their particular time and place as surely as is the ancient text. . . . It is not desirable, because the Bible can only be properly understood as it is read with a *participatory involvement* and allowed to speak into one's own situation. Ultimately, if the text written in the past does not strike home in the present it has not been understood.[6]

Of course, by "properly understood," Padilla refers to a specifically Christian reading of the Christian Bible, which, then, presupposes something other than a hermeneutics of detachment and disinterest.

Where this criticism of "objective biblical studies" has been resisted or rejected, it is usually because of difficulties surrounding the meaning of the term *objective*. The usual fear is that the alternative to *objective exegesis* (*exegesis*, from the Greek, *ex* + *geomai*: "to lead out of") of the Bible is *eisegesis* (*eisegesis*, from the Greek, *eis* + *geomai*: "to lead into"), that is, our reading "into" the biblical materials whatever we wanted the Bible to say in the first place. If this sort of "interested" biblical study is nothing more than conscripting the Bible for service in self-authorizing interpretation, then "disinterested" may seem to be the only reasonable alternative.

We may be helped by some terminological sanitation. The rejection of "objectivity" in biblical studies was never designed to devalue what Thomas Haskell calls "the elementary capacity for self-overcoming."[7] Fairness and honesty, a healthy recognition of one's convictions, and a capacity for self-reflexiveness are qualities we have every right to expect of one another. In fact, it might better be said that the sort of objectivity we want from one another is not only compatible with but is only possible when our commitments are recognized, laid bare, and open to scrutiny. The brand of "objectivity in biblical studies" worth resisting, then, is the quest for the holy grail of interpreter neutrality or, even worse, the claim that one has achieved it.

The way forward might be helped if we were to admit with Haskell that objectivity is not neutrality—that our capacity and need for self-overcoming does not entail a denial of our selves and our locations. "Self-overcoming" is not a prerequisite to good biblical interpretation but it may well be its outcome, as prior convictions are shaped in the communal give and take of reading the Bible as Scripture within the one, holy, catholic, and apostolic church. Accordingly, when I claim that reading the Bible as Scripture requires an ecclesial location, I am denying the possibility of interpretive neutrality, affirming the importance of identifying oneself with and among the community of faith, and insisting that this identity is not antithetical to the fairness, honesty, and respect we associate with intellectual discourse.

Someone may accuse me of thus redefining "intellectual discourse" or "academic study of the Bible"—an accusation to which, with one proviso, I will readily plead guilty. That proviso is this: I am not so much redefining as reclaiming; after all, it is only since the late-eighteenth century that one could argue that ecclesial commitments would of necessity marginalize a commitment to the intellect. Garrett Green lays responsibility for the mischief that bedevils us at the feet of G. W. F. Hegel, who at the turn of the nineteenth century rejected "the positivity of the Christian religion." By "positivity," Hegel referred to those teachings of the faith that were grounded in arbitrary appeal to the authority of specific historical figures and occurrences; this would become the basis for a distinction between *natural religion* (religion accessible through reason) and *positive religion* (based on religious authority, whether human or divine, and especially on Scripture and the classical creeds).[8] Accordingly, the intellectual study of the biblical materials would necessarily require that they be studied in some way other than as documents possessing or otherwise implicated in religious authority. It is against this neutering Christian Scripture of its power to engage the human person that I stand in claiming that reading Scripture is and can only be an ecclesially located enterprise.

In fact, the ecclesial location of our work with the Bible functions as an important constraint in our interpretive work. From Nietzsche, Freud, and Marx flows an awareness, highlighted in more recent times in cultural studies, of the ideological character of interpreters, traditions of interpretation, and interpretive communities. One need not adopt all of the particulars of these "purveyors of doubt" to acknowledge with them something of the degree to which we read from our own histories, commitments, and concerns. We cannot escape the clothing of our own experiences as we take up the task of biblical interpretation—a reality that is both boon and bane in our engagement with Scripture. In my own classes, I have witnessed the profound, serendipitous insight medical professionals bring to the interpretation of some texts; given their training and background, they simply see things and pursue questions that would never have occurred to me. Similarly, I am sure, their training and background blind them to other aspects of the text, aspects on which the spotlight might settle in a group of lawyers, a group of the elderly, or a group of refugees.

Self-consciously bringing ourselves with us to the work of reading Scripture comes with its advantages. It helps us come clean with our commitments and concerns, the interests that shape our reading of these texts, helping us approach our interpretive work more honestly. This renders our experiences and commitments more easily accessible to critical scrutiny and transformation when our life-worlds are unveiled as parochial or egocentric.

However, if the indispensable and unavoidable point of departure for the practice of reading the Bible is the set of particulars that comprise us as persons, the question remains whether these texts will be domesticated by our commitments, our life-worlds. In this regard, the ecclesial location of our engaging with Scripture can function as a corrective. This assumes, of course, that we have been formed in such dispositions as acceptance, devotion, attention, trust, and hospitality. One of the most tragic effects of Bible reading can be that we read our lives into it in such a way that we find in its pages divine license for those of our attitudes and practices that are more base than biblical. Our experience is too often that we apply challenging messages to the lives of others while assuming too quickly that the Bible supports our ways of thinking and acting. We read Scripture in order to be addressed by God and formed by his Word. Other people set on the same purpose can serve to take us to task so that we might hear more faithfully God's voice at those moments when we are tempted to exchange for God's Word a word of our own.

Locating our reading of Scripture within the ecclesial community immediately reconfigures the range of voices we allow to shape us.

> **One of the most tragic effects of Bible reading can be that we read our lives into it in such a way that we find divine license for those of our attitudes and practices that are more base than biblical.**

We may be tempted to listen only to a venerated teacher—say, one whose books are best sellers, whose church is packed, whose website has thousands of weekly hits. Less likely today, but possible, we may be tempted to listen only to the learned critical commentary, the one exhibiting the highest level of erudition. Or we may be tempted to listen only to the voice of the Holy Spirit, imagining that, on our own, we have direct access to the counsel of God with regard to the meaning of the Bible. Each in its own way is a mistaken path. The practice of reading the Bible as Scripture is an agenda for the whole faith community—including, to be sure, the voices of the trained, but also voices representing political commitments other than our own, theological traditions other than our own, ethnicities other than our own, stages of life other than our own, social and economic tiers other than our own, and historical ages other than our own. To whom do we listen? What voices do we privilege? Young voices? Inner-city voices? What have we to learn from our grandmothers' readings of Scripture? From the emerging church's readings of Scripture? From the "other" end of the political spectrum, whether the Left or the Right, whether Red or Blue? What might we learn from the church in Bosnia or Bogotá? From Irenaeus or Bede or Wesley? How might we be blind and deaf to the voice of God in these texts apart from our hearing what the Spirit is saying to the church through our Christian sisters and brothers from other times and places?

If we are to have readerly interests (and we do) *and* remain open to the challenge of these texts to which we turn as Scripture, we will need continually to adopt a position of openness to the Christian community within which we read them. The church historic and global is our conversation partner in the hermeneutical task. Interpreters who are manifestly "not like us" can assist us in hearing those melodies in Scripture for which we would otherwise have no ear.

Reading Scripture Must Be Theologically Fashioned

No neutral ledge exists on which we might stand to engage seriously the biblical materials. We inevitably bring with us our own interests and commitments. Although a variety of interests are possible and perhaps defensible, a reading of the Bible as Christian Scripture can never be satisfied with anything less than interpretive practices oriented toward shaping and nurturing the faith and life of God's people. The implications of this are several, three of which I want to sketch here: (1) the import of the Old Testament, (2) the reading of Scripture as a "ruled reading," and (3) the significance of locating one's community within its theological tradition.

1. Briefly to reiterate an earlier concern,[9] it is essential that Christian study of the Old Testament interpret these writings specifically as Christian Scripture and that the New Testament be firmly situated within the grand narrative of God's purpose that is incomprehensible apart from the Old Testament. If the "main character" of the Bible is God, then it is God, and his purpose, who unifies the Old and New Testaments, and we dare not imagine that we have understood or might begin to understand the significance of Jesus Christ if we have not acquainted ourselves with the God whom he worshiped and addressed as "Father."

2. The church's doctrine provides, as it were, the rules of engagement in a reading of Scripture. This may be a difficult claim for children of the Reformation, for whom the relation of the biblical text to the theological tradition presents an unresolved and inescapable conundrum. The same may be said for children of the Enlightenment. The slogan *sola Scriptura* raises the question, How does Scripture function vis-à-vis doctrine, the teaching office of the church, experience, and so on? Similarly the hegemony of human inquiry over all other forms of authority, doctrine included, raises the question whether theological statements from another time have bearing on our own (thus, the crest of England's Royal Society from the seventeenth century: *nullius in verba*, "on the word of no one"). The troubled relationship between Scripture and theology has admirable roots, to be sure. The sixteenth- and seventeenth-century need to wrestle the Bible from dogmatic clutches was a real one, but today biblical and theological studies seem not to speak the same language and, in ways more pervasive than often realized, biblical studies is still guided by an apprehensiveness toward a potential theological or ecclesial misapplication or misuse of the biblical witness. As a rule, biblical scholars are wary of theological categories and doctrinal systems that might predetermine what the Bible can or cannot say. To be avoided at all costs is the anachronistic theological framework into which the pluriform message of Scripture might be squeezed. As a result, theology today often seems quite capable of carrying on its work sans any need to draw on or check in with biblical studies, and vice versa.

For this reason, we need to struggle again with the doctrinal context of a reading of the Bible as Scripture—and particularly, the claim that a reading of Scripture worthy of the name "Christian" is necessarily a "ruled reading." That is, the question of validity in interpretation for theological readings of Scripture cannot be separated from the question of a particular reading's coherence with classical faith. Noting the need to move beyond the insights of Scripture in order to face challenges addressed to subsequent Christian communities, Alister McGrath observes the concern in the early centuries of the church to extend the biblical vocabulary and conceptual framework in ways consonant with Scripture's central insights. The consequence—those doctrinal formulations that would interpret (and not merely restate) biblical traditions concerning Jesus—was doctrine, which functions to define communities of discourse.[10]

McGrath's formulation might be read as a concern with the limitations of Scripture. The opposite is more to the point. The presenting issue is actually the polysemy of the biblical materials, their surplus of meaning. Biblical texts, taken on their own terms and without recourse to a history or community of interpretation, are capable of supporting multiple interpretations, and it becomes clear that, even if we want to affirm that engagement with the Bible is an inescapable quality of the Christian community, *sola Scriptura* can never guarantee that one is Christian. Irenaeus (ca. 130–ca. 202), for example, noted how Gnostics made use of biblical exegesis in their arguments, but insisted that they did not read the Scriptures aright on account of their disregard of the "order and connection" of Scripture. Failing to understand the Bible's true content, they put the pieces of the biblical puzzle together in a way that turned a royal personage into a hound or fox (*Adversus Haereses* 1.8.1). The "order and connection" to which Irenaeus referred was the rule of truth (sometimes called a "rule of faith"), a summary of the Christian kerygma that measured faithful interpretation of Scripture. Writing of this stage in the church's history, William Abraham observes:

> The development of a scriptural canon was utterly inadequate to meet the challenge posed by the Gnostics. The Gnostics had no difficulty accepting any canon of Scripture which might be proposed; being astute in their own way and eclectic in their intellectual sensibilities, they simply found ways to use Scripture to express their own theological convictions. *This should come as no surprise to anyone. A list of diverse books merely by the sheer volume involved is susceptible to a great variety of readings.*[11]

In early patristic exegesis, the notion of "economy" was paramount, for the correct interpretation of Scripture must express its economy, that is, its overall order or structure. For Irenaeus and others, "The true and accurate reading of scripture . . . must follow the divine economy by which God has put together the mosaic of scripture."[12] This perspective is not reserved to the church's dawning years. In the last century, Barth urged that the "whole" within which the parts of the Bible must be comprehended was its unified witness to God.[13] The earliest creedal traditions (already at work in the earliest New Testament documents, for example, from the simple acclamation, "Jesus is Lord" [1 Cor. 12:1] to more developed formulas such as we find in 1 Cor. 15:3-5) served to unify the Christian movement and to clarify its faith in the context of its challengers, with the result that the ecumenical creeds speak to the integrity of the Christian church and its faith. "The creed provides a measure or rule for the proper reading of Scripture," writes Luke Johnson.

"Such a rule is necessary for a coherent communal understanding of Scripture."[14]

Let me propose, however, that more needs to be said, that the relationship between Scripture and doctrine needs to be viewed at least to some degree in terms of mutual influence. A brief discussion of three such areas will suggest how the voice of Scripture needs to be heard more sonorously than too narrow an emphasis on the creedal tradition might allow. First, taking the Apostles' Creed as an exemplar, it is puzzling that, in its witness to our confession of Jesus' role as Savior and Lord, the creed summarizes one of our central beliefs in a rather one-sided representation of the return of Christ: "from thence he shall come to judge the quick and the dead."[15] Not least in modern Western culture, where guilt plays so large a role in our collective personality, images of "Christ the Judge" may not be entirely welcome, even among those who have turned to Jesus in faith. Even among Christians, "judgment" may evoke feelings less of hope than of fear. It is therefore always worth remembering that "judgment" does not simply refer to "condemnation," but has to do more broadly with assessment and division, so that some might with good reason anticipate judgment as the time when they and their cause will be vindicated. It is also worth remembering who will pronounce final judgment. The End will be marked by judgment, to be sure, but this is the judgment exacted by the one who "came to seek out and to save the lost" (Luke 19:10). Even after granting these interpretive provisos, however, it is remarkable that the creed can speak of the coming judgment without bearing more explicit witness to the consummation of God's purpose in creation and covenant, and, indeed, to the biblical hope of the restoration of the cosmos. The creed's witness thus stands in need of augmentation.

Second, it is enigmatic that the significance of Jesus' life can be passed over so easily in the space between the two affirmations, "born of the Virgin Mary, suffered under Pontius Pilate." That the New Testament devotes four of its books to narrations of Jesus' ministry registers a level of importance that seems overlooked by the creed. Moreover, those repeated appeals to "the faithfulness of Jesus"[16] in the New Testament letters presume some significance to the shape of the life of Jesus of Nazareth. Again, however, this is not suggested by the creed—a lacuna that has repercussions both for Christology (and especially for our understanding of Jesus' sonship) and for discipleship (i.e., for those who "follow the example of Jesus").

Third, the creedal traditions have nothing to say of Israel. It might be urged that the tradition should not be expected to mention something so pervasive to the Bible as the import of Israel in the divine economy. This argument lacks traction, however, since the creed does mention from the Old Testament the one thing that might most easily be taken for granted, namely, the work of God in creation ("I believe in God . . . maker of heaven and earth"). Instead, we cannot escape the need in the first three centuries of the Common Era for Christians to work out their self-identity especially with respect to Judaism, and that they often did so in contradistinction to Judaism. Yet, it is worth noting that, for Luke and Paul, to name two prominent New Testament theologians, the narrative of God's purpose cannot circumnavigate Israel and fully remain the biblical narrative, whereas the "confessional documents" of the Christian church seem to have written Israel out of the story altogether. Here, again, we have evidence that doctrine cannot simply trump the work of biblical interpretation but must be placed in a dialectical relationship with Scripture that is mutually informing.

3. The third consequence of an emphasis on a theologically fashioned reading of the Scripture is its recognition that, as Christians, we read out of a tradition. Locating our reading of Scripture in the church, we are reminded that, whether we know or admit it, all of us are reared, to some degree or another, within a particular ecclesial and theological tradition. As a "methodist,"[17] for example, I am heir to a tradition within which the importance of theological formation for biblical interpretation is a nonnegotiable.

At first blush, the nature of John Wesley's appeal to Scripture seems straightforward enough: "Bring me plain, scriptural proof for your assertion, or I cannot allow it."[18] Apparently to his detractors, Wesley's commitments regarding Scripture went beyond straightforward to simplistic, even base; note the derisive labels directed at him and his movement: Bible-bigots, Bible-moths, and the like.[19] In the theological world of Wesley's construction, however, "plain, scriptural proof," "plain truth for plain people," and "the plain sense of Scripture" comprised important hermeneutical mottos whose significance ought not be tied simply to Wesley's high view of Scripture. Indeed, the higher the view of Scripture, the more central and, perhaps, controvertible are issues of interpretation, since willingness to stand under Scripture presses all the more questions regarding what the Scriptures say. Hence, when Wesley and his methodists speak of the plain meaning of Scripture, we must ask, *Plain to whom?* What sort of people would hear the message of Scripture in just this way?

Like those of the Protestant Reformation before him, Wesley moved away from the four senses of Scripture characteristic of much medieval exegesis in favor of "the plain, literal meaning." "You are in danger of enthusiasm every hour," he wrote, "if you depart ever so little from Scripture; yea, or from the plain, literal meaning of any text, taken in connection with the context."[20] We would be mistaken, however, were we to imagine that Wesley argued for a reading of Scripture focused on "context" as this has been defined in subsequent biblical scholarship—either as historical context or literary context. When modern folk complain that, in his approach to Scripture, Wesley was "precritical," they appear to be denying Wesley's membership in the guild of modern, historical criticism; however mistaken in their truncated use of the term *critical*, at least they are right on this score: Wesley was not a modern historical or literary critic.

What, then, might it mean to learn from Wesley? First, to some significant degree, what it means to engage in a Wesleyan reading of Scripture is that those doing the reading have been nurtured in the Wesleyan tradition of according privilege to some theological categories over others, particularly, the pursuit of holiness and the primacy of grace—"holy love" as Ken Collins has framed it.[21] From this perspective, reading is less "discovery of meaning" and more theologically formed "performance" of Scripture. We read with a constant eye to "the Scripture way of salvation," and we do so in ways oriented toward the ongoing formation of the people of God in holiness. We do not claim for our readings as Wesleyans a completeness of meaning, or that they constitute the only possible ways of construing texts. We do exhibit in our lives, though, how, from within *this* community of reading, we hear and embody these patterns of words in distinctive keys. Neither does this theological approach sanction every reading as equally valid, but it does indicate in one significant way how diverse readings of the same text might lay claim to legitimacy.

Second, with regard to Wesley's interest in a "literal sense," it is important to remember that, for Wesley, this "sense" of Scripture was grounded, above all, in the intent of Scripture's one author— God. This, not incidentally, is why methodists generally are not prone to tying their faith to particular biblical phrases or exegesis of particular, carefully chosen verses. The whole is greater than the sum of the parts, since it is as a whole that the intent of Scripture's divine author is best on display. Accordingly, the "literal sense" of a text must coincide with the general tenor of Scripture. In other words, the meaning of biblical texts might be said to be "plain" when placed within the context of the whole of Scripture's message, which Wesley understood in especially soteriological (that is, salvation-oriented) terms. Although it is more usual today to speak of the "drama of Scripture" in terms of the overarching, canonical narrative running from Genesis to Revelation, creation to new creation, even more pivotal for Wesley was the soteriological progress of God's people, the narrative of coming to faith and moving on to perfection. Thus, for Wesley, the purpose of biblical interpretation is singular, as he writes at the opening of his *Sermons on Several Occasions*:

> I want to know one thing, the way to heaven,—how to land safe on that happy shore. God himself has condescended to teach the way: for this very end he came from heaven. He hath written it down in a book. O give me that book! At any price give me the Book of God! I have it. Here is knowledge enough for me. Let me be *homo unius libri*. Here then I am, far from the busy ways of men. I sit down alone: only God is here. In his presence I open, I read his Book; for this end, to find the way to heaven.[22]

We may stumble over these words and miss their force. We might take offense at this apparent reduction of the gift of salvation to life after death, as though heaven were the single, narrow locus of salvation. We might be annoyed by what we hear as hints of an insidious individualism, as though Bible reading or otherwise charting the "way to heaven" was something one might do on one's own, alone with God. It is important to recall, then, the horizons of Wesley's larger message and program, with its profoundly social understanding of church and attendant focus on mutual accountability, relational growth in grace, and communal participation and discernment. Moreover, Wesley deploys the phrase "the way to heaven" not to restrict salvation to life in the hereafter, but to speak of the life journey as a whole, a "way" marked by growth in grace and faithfulness, a journey whose beginning, middle, and end are mapped in relation to God and God's people. Accordingly, we hear in Wesley's words two pivotal emphases: salvation is a "way," a journey, a life path, and not only or merely a point in time or a destination we seek; and this way of salvation is the theme of Scripture. Salvation, then, is Scripture's organizing principle and is therefore the theological context within which the Bible is to be read,[23] as well as its essential aim.

Reading Scripture
Must Be Critically Engaged

By *critical*, I refer to the need for discernment with reference to the varieties of possible readings of biblical texts. In doing so, I am not wanting to accord privilege to one particular criterion for adjudicating competing readings of the one text. Nor am I desirous of opening myself to the charge of *presentism*, that is, the arrogant presumption that only those forms of inquiry characteristic of or found useful in the modern era are worthy of the label *critical*. In spite of attempts by some to divide history into three ages—precritical, critical, and postcritical—we ought to recognize that each people has its own orientation to critical engagement.[24]

Biblical interpretation today is faced with a critical challenge. A Chinese feminist theologian such as Kwok Pui-lan can invite forms of hermeneutical inquiry indigenous to Asia and Asian women while at the same time rejecting "Western" modes of reading because of their roots in the matrix of the alien, Western intellectual tradition.[25] Gerald West, however, can inquire into what hermeneutical approach would release Scripture as a truly liberating force in South Africa's black community.[26] Similar illustrations abound, documenting the keen influence of contextual location and readerly presupposition in practices of biblical interpretation. For some, it is only one small step from one's awareness of such conflicted, even competing interests to a hermeneutic that might best be described as "reactive." Recognizing that no reading is innocent or devoid of ideology, such readers formulate the interpretive experience as a battleground whereby readers seek to overthrow the perspectives of both the text and the history of its interpretation in order to replace them with their own.[27]

Considerations of this kind raise important questions. Can biblical texts function as anything more than mirrors of our own cultural presuppositions? Are we able to find in the Bible only that for which we had gone looking? Is "meaning" something only to be imposed? How might we arbitrate competing readings of the same text?

These are portentous questions, especially given the ease with which religious communities historically have found in their readings of Scripture divine legitimation for sometimes-heinous practices. One has only to reflect on traditions of biblical interpretation that have undergirded apartheid in South Africa, classism in Britain, the treatment of Native Americans in the United States, or the almost global disparaging of women, to name only four cases, in order to recognize the need for critical engagement.

I have emphasized that to read the Bible as Scripture is to leave open at every turn the possibility that our interpretive traditions are erroneous and in need of reformation. As Hans-Georg Gadamer argues:

> A person trying to understand something will not resign himself from the start to relying on

To read the Bible as Scripture is to leave open, at every turn, the possibility that our interpretive traditions are erroneous and in need of reformation.

his own accidental fore-meanings, ignoring as consistently and stubbornly as possible the actual meaning of the text until the latter becomes so persistently audible that it breaks through what the interpreter imagines it to be. Rather a person trying to understand a text is prepared for it to tell him something. That is why a hermeneutically trained consciousness must be, from the start, sensitive to the text's alterity.[28]

We come to Scripture again and again, in humility, not only with our questions but with an openness to its questions—open to the possibility that this text will speak a word over against us and our interpretive communities.

Of course, all reading is shaped by external commitments and our explicit recognition of the commitments of our reading communities is a positive response to the reality that the Word of God is always scandalous in its specificity. The Word of God came to John in the wilderness at a certain time, in the context of a particular politico-religious framework (Luke 3:1-2). Paul wrote to the Corinthians, a particular people in a particular place at a particular time for particular reasons. Even if the gospel embraces the whole cosmos and is universal in its claims, life in light of the gospel is lived by persons in economically deprived southeast Dallas, on wheat farms in Kansas, and in the suburbs of Cincinnati.

Recognition of the incarnation of God's Word does not open the way for each local congregation or interpretive tradition to have its own private interpretation. Nor is it to deny the wisdom of a teaching office at supralocal levels of church life. The particularity of revelation requires engagement with Scripture at the local level and within communities of God's people, but also counters the development of tunnel vision—ingrown and unself-critical faith. Part of the critical task is the involvement of congregations in conversation with biblical interpretation among others seeking to be faithful disciples—across time and across lines of all kinds, be they generational, urban or suburban or rural, gender-related, racial, national, political, and so on. Local instantiations of the Body of Christ need the whole Body of Christ, global and historical, in order to remain open to the scriptural voices not usually heard.

In short, the practice of reading Scripture, if it is to be critically engaged, must take seriously a range of conversation partners. Ultimately, a hermeneutic capable of addressing the sorts of concerns I have sketched must have a "discursive" profile. That is, it must attend to a range of overlapping and interlocking levels of discourse—some represented by and in the biblical texts themselves, some related to the history and contemporary practice of biblical interpretation, and some that take seriously the location of the church within the world created and redeemed by God. Critically engaged conversation would be:

- *Cross-cultural:* taking seriously the contexts both within which these texts were generated and within which contemporary interpretation takes place, in order to inhibit the wholesale cultural imperialism that surfaces when we assume all people everywhere and in all times think, believe, and act like us (or me);
- *Canonical:* taking seriously how the canon comprises a diversity of voices that balance and counterbalance one another, yet presents itself as the unitary self-disclosure of the one God who created the cosmos, called and liberated

a people, sent God's son and raised him from the dead, poured out the Spirit, and who is now moving the cosmos toward its *telos*;

- *Historical:* taking seriously that we are not the first persons to read Scripture, that our own readings of Scripture are, for good or bad, shaped by previous interpreters, and that our mothers and fathers in the faith have much to contribute to our formation as persons who embody and bear witness to the gospel;
- *Communal:* taking seriously that Scripture is itself concerned with the formation of the community of God's people and that biblical interpretation, in order to be authentically *biblical* in this sense, is the work of that community;
- *Global:* taking seriously that our faith communities are themselves subject to the cultivation of private and idiosyncratic interpretations, and thus need the witness of ecclesial communities "not like ours" as conversation partners; and
- *Hospitable:* taking seriously that, even as God's grace extends to all people, we may learn from those whose lives seem not at all to be oriented around God—persons, then, who may be able to remedy our tendencies toward interpretive arrogance.

If the hermeneutical agenda thus outlined seems daunting, this is understandable. This is not cause for despair, however, but rather reminds us that the performance of Scripture is a lifelong journey and that engaging the Scriptures is the activity of the church and not only that of an individual, as well as provides whatever impetus is necessary for the cultivation among ourselves of such dispositions as openness and humility. Our need for one another—people in Southern and Northern hemispheres, churches in the East and West, communities past and present, and so on—has never been more apparent.

Reading Scripture Must Be Spirit-imbued

Discussions of biblical inspiration are fond of drawing attention to the ongoing role of the Holy Spirit in the processes of the generation, canonization, and transmission of biblical texts, and then in the interpretation of those texts. As important an affirmation as this is, how the Holy Spirit is thus involved is less easy to articulate. How do we talk about the role of the Holy Spirit in biblical interpretation? It is tempting to acknowledge that, like the Spirit, "the wind blows where it chooses, and you hear the sound of it, but you do not know where it comes from or where it goes" (John 3:8), celebrate the work of the Spirit as a mystery, and move on to the next topic. It is possible, though, to explore that mystery further, however incompletely. I will make four claims.

1. To invite the Holy Spirit into the interpretive process is to deny our autonomy as readers of Scripture and to affirm our dependence on the Spirit and on the community of God's people generated by the Spirit. According to the eminent philosopher Charles Taylor, such behavior on our part strikes at the root of our identities as

modern persons in the West. In *Sources of the Self*, Taylor sketches the development of modern identity from Augustine through Descartes, Locke, and Kant, and on into the Romantics. He finds that personal identity has come to be shaped by such assumptions, little acknowledged and little discussed, such as these: human dignity lies in self-sufficiency and self-determination; identity is grasped in self-referential terms: I am who I am; persons have an inner self, which is the authentic self; and basic to authentic personhood are self-autonomy and self-legislation.[29] To name the Bible as Christian Scripture is already to undercut this portrait, for this requires us both to recognize an authority outside of ourselves and, indeed, to parade that recognition before others. To seek the assistance of the Spirit in our reading of the Scriptures—our interpretation and embodiment of them—is even further to engage in a practice that flies in the face of our former, typically unspoken but tightly held, claims of self-sufficiency.

Acts 15 provides an important exemplar of the process of discernment around the Scriptures. The presenting question is whether Gentiles must undergo circumcision according to the custom of Moses in order to be saved (15:1, 5). The apostles and elders gather—first, to hear from Peter how the Spirit had testified to the salvation of the Gentiles "by giving them the Holy Spirit, just as he did to us; and in cleansing their hearts by faith he has made no distinction between them and us" (15:8-9); and then from Barnabas and Paul, whose testimony Luke summarizes only briefly, having just devoted two whole chapters (Acts 13–14) to the work of the Spirit among the Gentiles in their mission. Finally, James engages in

95

biblical interpretation—not by finding in the Scriptures a new revelation that was not already present in them, but, on account of the manifest witness of the Spirit in the apostolic mission, by attending to aspects of the biblical message that had been hidden in the shadows of the faith and life of God's people (15:13-18). The work of the Spirit thus prompted a second look at the witness of Scripture. On this basis, those gathered could write, "For it has seemed good to the Holy Spirit and to us" (15:28).

2. As the Holy Spirit is the divine agent of sanctification, so the Spirit is at work in shaping us for reading the Bible as Scripture, that is, with dispositions and posture of invitation, openness, and availability. An integrated life of devotion to God, conversational intimacy with God, our capacity to enter into prayer as submission, our willingness to participate in a repentance-oriented reading of Scripture—these orientations and concomitant practices are the fruit of the work of the Spirit in our lives.

Negatively, this emphasis on the role of the Spirit in inducting us into the conversation of heaven works against certain emphases in biblical interpretation in modern times. Attitudes of skepticism accompanying historical inquiry are eclipsed by an openness to the God for whom all things are possible. Minimalist approaches to the possible ways in which a biblical text might find significance in the divine economy are set aside in favor of an openness to the possible intentions of the divine author whose ways are higher than our ways, whose thoughts are higher than our thoughts (cf. Isa. 55:8-9). Accordingly, a Spirit-imbued reading of Scripture may appear to take risks when compared with those forms of modern, critical study wary of what might go wrong in the interpretive process. But this is a necessary risk, and our taking it is an expression of our trust in the Spirit not only to guide our interpretation, but also, over time, to direct the church in its interpretation and embodiment of Scripture. Discussing "the meaning of the Spirit," de Lubac warned:

> No matter what suppleness of mind is brought to determining this meaning, no matter what changes are rightly envisaged in the ways leading naturally to it, the Spirit of Christ cannot be omitted. It is a gift of this Spirit. In order to receive it, it is not enough, therefore, to "press hard," to "seek"; it is also necessary to "pray," to "implore." . . . For anyone who thinks he is able to do without the Spirit of God and yet uncover the Mysteries of Scriptures is exactly like a man who, without a light, loses his way and has only unfamiliar walls to touch.[30]

The Spirit teaches us to affirm *both* the knowability *and* unfathomability of God—the God who would be known and yet the God whose depths can never be plumbed.

3. As the Spirit of Christ was active in the generation of Scripture, so, in our actualization of the Scriptures, the Spirit points us to Christ. This affirmation presses us in various directions at once. We hear the long-standing theological affirmation that the Spirit is the "first author" of the Scriptures—the Spirit whose presence and activity pulls us into the life of the Triune God. We see the emphasis of Luke-Acts on prayer as the context within which the Spirit reveals the identity of Christ and the character of God's missional agenda—typically in contexts that involve the interpretation of the Scriptures (e.g., Luke 3:21-22; 9:18-27; Acts 1:15-26; 3:23-31; 9:32–11:18). We see the emphasis of 1 Peter on the Spirit of Christ who inspired the prophets and who is presently engaged in the

interpretation of the Scriptures (1:10-12). Peter's hermeneutic centers on the animating presence of the Spirit of Christ (see above, chapter 2). This is not because we are taught by the advent of Christ to read the Scriptures retrospectively; instead, the Christ whom Christians worship as Lord is the same Christ who long ago revealed the ways of God in the Scriptures. Together, Old and New Testaments therefore testify to the Christ who first inspired them. (Other references to the Spirit as the Spirit of Christ [or of Jesus, or of Jesus Christ] appear in Acts 16:7; Rom. 8:9; Phil. 1:19.)

The Spirit of Christ is none other than the Spirit at work in Jesus' life and mission. He was conceived by the Holy Spirit, anointed by the Spirit, and operated in the arena and with the power of the Spirit. This is the same Spirit who revealed Jesus' identity (Luke 3:21-22) and under whose influence Jesus identified himself with the words of Isaiah: "The Spirit of the Lord is upon me" (Luke 4:1-30; with reference to Isa. 58:6; 61:1-2). In Paul, the Spirit and Christ are related so forcefully that the two seem at times virtually to be identified. Here, then, is an important constraint on readings of the Christian Scriptures: whatever work is attributed to the Spirit, including the work of reading and embodying the Scriptures, is identifiable as an expression of Jesus of Nazareth, Christ, the Son of God, and so must conform to him.

4. The Spirit forms us as and within an interpretive community— the people of God continuous through history and across the globe. First, this disallows the notion of a "private" or individualized reading of the Bible and opens the path for participation by the whole people of God in the interpretive task and for the role of the whole

people of God, over time, in the work of authorizing some interpretations over others.[31]

This means, second, that we honor the history of biblical interpretation, the history of the effects of the church's engagement with its Scripture (sometimes known by the German word *Wirkungsgeschichte*), and the work of interpretation taking place in areas of the globe other than our own. These represent arenas of the Spirit's work among our mothers and fathers, sisters and brothers in the faith, whose interaction with the Bible is potentially formative of ours. For this reason, we can celebrate the publication of projects such as *Ancient Christian Commentary on Scripture* and *The Church's Bible*, which index for contemporary readers the classical tradition of biblical interpretation; and projects such as the *Global Bible Commentary*, which give voice to contemporary readings of Scripture from locales around the world.[32] Whatever their shortcomings, these publishing efforts begin to allow access more fully to what the Spirit is saying to the church in its particular locations (cf. Rev. 2–3).

Third, this entails our recognition of the significance of the tradition of the church, again as the arena in which the Spirit has been at work and, so, as an important means by which to discern the shape and substance of genuinely Christian interpretation.[33] In part, this is another affirmation that the "Scripture only" principle needs emendation in favor of an expansive notion of the place of the Bible in the life of the church, alongside other theological norms and practices. "Interpretation and realization of Scripture are ecclesiological events, and therefore the church and its tradition are integral to the handling of the Bible."[34] To proclaim the work of the Spirit in the ongoing life of the church is to recognize the importance of reading Scripture in relation to the historic faith of the church and those expressions of the church that have stood the test of time.

Conclusion

It will be obvious that, in its truest form, "study of the Bible" is not something that one does alongside other pursuits. Interpreting the Bible as Christian Scripture serves as the focal point of other disciplines, including historical theology or prayer, that is, of disciplinary nodes in the theological curricula in a seminary or school of theology as well as of the habits of faith and life that occupy Christians more generally. If one of the common models of the place of the Bible is as *foundation* (foundation of theology, foundation of the life of the church, and so forth), a more appropriate image might be the Bible as *center*, with spokes representative of the life and faith of God's people feeding into and emanating from its pages.

Another way to get at this would be to resist the popular image of Bible, church, work, worship, and theological training as circles on a page in search of connecting lines. Instead, these would occupy concentric circles, each fading into the next. Rather than recruiting, hiring, and training people to "build bridges" from biblical scholarship to communities of Christ's followers, we would set ourselves to the work of imagining what would happen were biblical studies to be located purposely and self-consciously *within* the church, just as the church is deliberate in its reflecting on the character of its Scripture-shaped identity and mission for the sake of the world.

Movement into these patterns of thought and practice are appropriate for those set on interpreting the Bible *as Scripture*, actualizing its message through incarnation within and among God's people. In order to help with this task, in this chapter I have drawn attention to some of the needed resources, encouraging a reading of Scripture that is ecclesially located, theologically fashioned, critically engaged, and Spirit imbued. Adopting this stance, we recall that *we* are the people of God to whom the Bible is addressed as Scripture, and we realize that the fundamental transformation that must take place is not the transformation of an ancient message into contemporary idiom but rather the transformation of our lives by means of God's Word. This means that reading the Bible as Scripture has less to do with what tools we bring to the task, however important these may be, and more to do with the location of our reading, the sensibilities that guide our conversations around these texts, and the dispositions by which we are drawn to Scripture.

CHAPTER FOUR

METHODS

ere we to conceive of the task of biblical interpretation along the lines we have sketched, what would our approach to actual biblical texts look like? Although my emphasis thus far on the formation of interpreters—that is, on the cultivation of a particular set of patterns of thinking, feeling, believing, and behaving—might encourage one to imagine that the hard work of exegetical analysis is unnecessary, this is hardly the case. If anything, a concern to read the Bible as Christian Scripture significantly raises the bar on what is and must be expected of the church. If we are to "understand" (that is, "stand under") these texts, if they are to have a peculiar, formative role in the life of those communities that regard them as Scripture, then *how these texts speak* is a matter of utmost importance.

Similarly, some might hear in my emphasis thus far on the "immediacy" of these scriptural texts, that is, their capacity to disclose the ways of God simultaneously to the one people of God instantiated in a variety of cultures across time and space, an attempt on my part to dispense with questions about method. As I have often been informed,

"Why all of this talk about *interpreting* the Bible? All you have to do is *read* it!" At the most basic level, however, these texts, like all texts, present challenges to their readers—challenges grounded simply in how they come to us, as linear forms of communication, selective in what they have to say, using sometimes ambiguous words and phrases. What is more, these texts derive from a different time and place than our own, speak of people and places unknown to us, and incorporate assumptions that sometimes escape us (see chapter 1). If, as the church believes, these texts mediated the divine voice in those times and places, the question remains, How might they function thus for us?

By way of addressing this question, I want, first, to map the terrain, so to speak. This will allow me to underscore the importance of method, mitigate the potentially exaggerated claims of any one method to be "the key" that unlocks the meaning of the text, and comment on why coming to the text from different angles is an important strategy. Second, I want to sketch a series of methodological concerns by advancing a number of interpretive questions and criteria. Third, I want to return to the problem of "technique" in the reading of Scripture, and urge that what we need are not so much better-honed methodological commitments and skills, but more fully developed interpretive sensibilities. To put it differently, reading the Bible as Christian Scripture is a craft that pleads for the lifelong apprenticeship of its artisans.

Getting the Lay of the Land

"Method" has to do with any of a range of interpretive strategies with which one might engage a text. In recent years, many students of the Bible have learned to catalogue these in terms of where each locates meaning in relation to the biblical text. Three (rather obvious) options have emerged:

- Behind the text
- In the text
- In front of the text

Behind-the-text approaches address the text as a window through which to access and examine the deposit of "meaning." These approaches, then, locate meaning in the history assumed by the text, the history that gave rise to the text, and/or the history to which a text gives witness. *In-the-text* methods recalibrate their gaze so as to bring into focus the qualities of the text itself, its architecture, consistency, and texture. Emphasis falls on the perspective contained within and transmitted by the text, apprehending the text as a kind of sealed "container" of meaning. *In-front-of-the-text* approaches orient themselves around the perspectives of various readers of the text, on readerly communities, and/or on the effects that texts (might) have on their readers. In this case, readers do not simply perceive but actually produce, or at least assist in the production of, meaning.

Two introductory comments need to be made about this typology. First, as I have expressed them, these are "ideal types" that rarely, if ever, appear in such pure forms. This has always been true to some degree, but is today even more so, since growing recognition of the potential of all of these approaches has fueled attempts to integrate them. Second, nevertheless, this typology continues to have utility, since our methods align themselves more with one category than another according to our particular philosophical comments about the location of meaning. Where do we locate meaning? What do we regard as authoritative? The history behind the text? The text itself? Those persons and communities doing the reading? Even those who want to reply "All three!" typically prioritize one over the others.

To anticipate, the answer I will sketch is "All three" while placing interpretive priority on the text itself—or, rather, on the capacity of the text (as cultural product and as Scripture) to trump the (ecclesially located) reader in the ongoing negotiation of meaning between text and reader. Before developing my response, though, I need to provide a map of the options.

1. *Behind the text*: Contemporary concern with method cannot be painted without reference to the enormous upheavals that have shaken the foundations of biblical study in the last forty years. During these decades, we have witnessed the fall of historical criticism as the approach that quite literally defined critical biblical studies. Accordingly, the two notions, usually held in tandem, that the meaning of a text is contained within its history and that the role of the interpreter is to isolate the one, single, historically intended, correct meaning of a biblical text have become increasingly marginal in biblical studies.

In New Testament studies, for example, historical questions have focused above all on the Gospels and Acts, narratives imagined by many readers to represent what really happened (or not) in the life and mission of Jesus and subsequently of his followers. That the New Testament includes four Gospels that, generally speaking, tell much the same story but differ at many points of detail and emphasis raised historical questions almost from the beginning.[1] According to Eusebius, Clement of Alexandria (ca. AD 150–220) accounted for the differences among the Gospels by observing that Matthew, Mark, and Luke recounted the "physical" facts while John composed a "spiritual Gospel" (*Hist. Eccl.* 6.14.7). Similarly, Origen, writing ca. 250 of the discrepancies between the Gospel of John and the synoptic Gospels, concluded, "I conceive it to be impossible for those who admit nothing more than the history in their interpretation to show that these discrepant statements are in harmony with each other" (*Commentary* 10.15)—a conclusion that cleared the way for Origen's use of additional methods in study of the Gospels.

In modern times, serious challenges to the historical veracity of the Gospels, as well as the New Testament as a whole, have come from discoveries of additional texts from antiquity, both Jewish and Christian, especially at Nag Hammadi and Qumran. Together, these findings reveal a breadth of diversity within the Judaism of Jesus' day (thus, the increasingly popular reference to "Judaisms") and within the Christian movement's first centuries not easily discerned from the pages of the New Testament. As a result, the relatively monochromatic portrait of "the Jews" and the relative priority of Pauline Christianity found generally in the New Testament have come under increasing scrutiny. Discovery of extant Christian documents or reconsideration of previously known documents have also raised questions about the sources appropriate for historical study of Jesus and the Christian movement. Noncanonical gospels (such as the Gospel of Thomas or the Gospel of Peter) are sometimes championed as containing material with historical priority over or at least along-side that found in the New Testament Gospels.

These challenges demonstrate how important historical issues have been in study of the Gospels. This is neither a new emphasis nor one confined to the halls of academia. Readers of the Gospels have long tended to read them as if they present the past, unadorned. This is further evidence for the more or less pervasive practice of behind-the-text approaches to biblical studies.

Key scholarly assumptions about history and historical inquiry have guided the conversation in modern times. First, in an attempt to provide methodological rigor to the study of the historical Jesus at the turn of the twentieth century, Ernst Troeltsch articulated three principles: the historicity of a reported event cannot be assumed (skepticism), the probability of a past event is determined by analogy with the occurrence of a similar event today (analogy), and every historical event is the effect of a historical cause (correlation). The effect of these widely adopted principles was to assess the historicity of ancient reports according to modern sensibilities, to rule out of court the possibility of the supernatural or miraculous, and to locate the burden of proof on any claim favoring historical veracity. Subsequent inquiry generated increasingly sophisticated criteria for use in evaluating the historicity of events recorded in the Gospels and Acts.

Second, since these historical methods and practices developed largely from the late-ninteenth through the mid-twentieth century, they generally reflect the reigning philosophy of history famously articulated by Leopold von Ranke (1795–1886). Not wanting to pass judgment on the past, he wanted simply to report "*wie es eigentlich gewesen*": "as it actually was." Historical inquiry in this tradition has long outlived von Ranke, motivated especially by a desire to emulate the investigative commitments and techniques of the natural sciences. Even if the philosophy of history has moved far beyond this vision of the historical project, this general approach has continued to influence New Testament studies.[2]

The staying power of these assumptions and the approach they fueled is extraordinary, as evidenced above all in the public popularity of life-of-Jesus research. In fact, in spite of serious questions raised against behind-the-text approaches to biblical studies, many in our churches and the American public more generally know no other way of thinking about the significance of Jesus. Who Jesus really was, what Jesus really thought of himself, and who really were included among Jesus' closest associates—such titillating questions have in recent years occupied the front covers of national news magazines and prompted television documentaries. This is fascinating since (1) the church looks to the Gospels as authoritative witnesses to the one gospel, who is Jesus Christ, and not to the Jesus reconstructed by even our best historians; (2) employing redaction, composition, and narrative criticisms, study of the Gospels in the past five or six decades has turned its attention more and more to the Gospels as witnesses to the significance of Jesus (and not as windows through which to recover "the real Jesus"); (3) we find little agreement among those who engage in historical Jesus research regarding criteria by which to determine what is or is not historical; and, (4) even with this variety of approaches, those attempts to recover the past characterizing most efforts at studying the historical Jesus are simply out of step with how history is now studied (that is, after a century of developments in the philosophy of history).[3]

An evaluation of behind-the-text approaches to the biblical materials would include other concerns as well. For example, contemporary philosophy of history promotes renewed interest with the *narrative character* of representations of historical events and with the rhetorical effects of those narratives. This includes recognition that history-writing provides us with both more and less than the past—more in that historiography construes events in a web of causal relationships that draw out a significance that is greater than individual episodes might suggest on their own, less in that historians must make ruthless decisions about what to exclude lest the retelling become infinitely detailed. History writing, then, is inherently *partial*: providing only a minute segment of the episodes that comprise the past, and doing so according to the inescapably subjective aims of the historian. In addition, history writing is a rhetorical exercise in which documentation and interpretation (or signification) are inextricably woven together. Events, which we experience serially as occurrences and situations, acquire a narrative form (arranging what has happened in a web of causation and meaning) that is unavoidably perspectival. Thus, in an important sense, all historiography is contemporary, since the historian demonstrates through narrative representation how the present grows organically out of sequences of past events. As a consequence, historiography serves powerfully the needs of community legitimation and validation, identity formation, and instruction. These kinds of considerations invite historical inquiry to address fresh questions—questions that eclipse a narrow focus on "what actually happened." These would include: What choices? What order? What perspective? What organizing principle? What overarching purpose?[4] To a remarkable degree, of course, these are questions that invite perspectives from narrative studies, an in-the-text mode of study.

This means that a good portion of what has passed for biblical studies in the past has proved to be shortsighted. The set of concerns usually associated with historical inquiry—recovering or reconstructing historical events, discerning the place of those events in antiquity, and tracing their transmission up to their inclusion within the narrative texts of the Bible—is ill-equipped to address the significance allotted these events in the memories and rhetoric of the communities in which they came to be written down in these forms. It remained for literary critics, then, to remind us that "facts" can be construed in a variety of meaningful frameworks, or that the narration of events is one of the most potent instruments in the arsenal of marginal peoples struggling with their identity and purpose as a people.[5]

Finally, we should account for the notable expansion of historical concerns through the influx into biblical studies of social-scientific interests and approaches. This includes heightened interest in social description (filling in the blanks of our knowledge of the details of everyday life in antiquity) as well as the application of sociological and cultural anthropological models to the world of the biblical materials. These take seriously the embodiment of human behavior and the ritual character of persons in community.[6]

In the waning years of the twentieth century, then, the foundations of historical study have been shaken rigorously. Nevertheless, the importance of history for biblical studies is incontestable, and not only because a number of the books of the Bible *look like* history writing, that is, they adopt modes of discourse congruent with ancient traditions of historiography (e.g., the Chronicles, the Gospels, and Acts). Additionally, God's people look to their God both as Creator and as One vitally engaged in the goings-on of the world. To cite a pivotal example, they point to God's decisive intervention in Exodus and the giving of the Law as the basis of their existence as a people. What is more, every New Testament document situates itself in history, whether localized to a city or region or even a particular household (e.g., Phil. 4:2; Philem.; Rev. 2–3) or worldwide in its scope (e.g., Luke 2:1-7; 3:1-6; 1 Pet. 5:9). The historical dimension of the Bible is further, decisively, documented in this central theological declaration: "The Word became flesh and lived among us, and we have seen his glory, the glory as of a father's only son, full of grace and truth" (John 1:14).

Hence, we could hardly call for the suspension or rejection of historical inquiry. Nevertheless, it is clear that we need more nuanced ways of construing notions of "history" and "historical." And we need forms of interpretation that highlight aspects of the text in addition to those historical events and traditions to which these texts give testimony.

2. *In the text*: For a brief period and in only selected quarters it appeared that the hyperconcern with historical issues that characterized critical scholarship since the nineteenth century might be

replaced with a narrow emphasis on the text itself. If, according to the historical critical paradigm, the meaning of a text cannot be equated with how it affects the reader ("The Affective Fallacy"), according to the literary turn in interpretation, neither can reports of an author's original intention be regarded as germane to criticism ("The Intentional Fallacy"). With this, many students of the Bible redoubled their efforts at finding meaning in texts.

In the case of the biblical writings, we should add that we are physically incapable of checking our interpretations against the intentions of their writers; indeed, in some cases, we do not even know to whom we should attribute the authorship of biblical texts. In the end, readers have only the text itself to consult. The effect of this truism was, for some interpreters, that the text itself could and ought to be regarded as a self-sufficient, self-contained verbal artifact. Accordingly, the text is presumed to be the unique and privileged source of meaning and interpretive value, with this available to the interpreter by means of careful attention to its language and structure.

For those concerned with reading the Bible as Christian Scripture, this forceful emphasis on the text itself is an important one. This is because, when Christians speak of inspiration and authority, they tend to refer above all to the text; after all, 2 Timothy 3:16 has it that "all scripture is inspired by God [or God-breathed]." Although one might refer to reconstructions of the historical Moses or of the historical Jesus as "inspiring," we do not regard them as "inspired," "God-breathed." Similarly, though we can refer to the work of the Holy Spirit in shaping and empowering readers of Scripture (see chapter 3), we do not typically refer to their readings as "inspired" in this more limited sense of the word.

Nevertheless, this approach has some glaring weaknesses. First, texts are not self-sufficient verbal artifacts that contain within themselves all that is needed for their interpretation. Claude Lévi-Strauss had spoken of a work of art as "an object endowed with precise properties, that must be analytically isolated, and this work can be entirely defined on the grounds of such properties." He urged that we approach the object of our interpretation "as an object which, once created, had the stiffness—so to speak—of a crystal; we [confine] ourselves to bringing into evidence these properties." Contradicting this perspective, Umberto Eco observed, "A text is not a 'crystal.' If it were a crystal, the cooperation of the reader would be part of its molecular structure."[7] For Eco, a text not only calls for the cooperation of its reader in the construction of meaning, but also summons the reader to make a series of interpretive choices.

Second, the biblical texts did not fall out of the sky; they are not facsimiles from heaven, but arose in particular times and places in response to particular situations. They are cultural products that participate in, legitimate, perpetuate, criticize, and so forth the worlds within which they were generated. Texts exist in a relationship of constraint and mobility with their cultural contexts as authors assemble and shape the forces of their worlds in fresh ways that both draw upon and point beyond those cultural elements.[8] Biblical texts have ongoing significance in part because of their capacity to speak beyond the limitations of their own historical particularity. Yet, as "cultural products," the fullness of their voice is determined by that very particularity. Attempts to understand these texts without reference to the cultural settings within which they took shape are like strapping on skates and moving out onto the ice with both hands tied behind our backs.

Third, not least when read as Christian Scripture, biblical texts do more than incorporate vestiges of the circumstances of their generation; they also refer beyond themselves. They cannot be reduced to self-referential, self-validating artifacts, for they point to a truth beyond themselves. They work to induct the believing community into this truth; they invite people to make their home within it, and, among those who do, Scripture forms a community that embodies this truth.

Unfortunately, the "truth" to which Scripture refers was in previous times reduced to determinations regarding the accuracy of these texts measured in terms of historical detail. As a result of the centuries of historical inquiry that ensued, some interpreters withdrew from historical forms of analysis altogether, preferring a restricted interest in the forms of the literary text. For some, this was a strategy for safeguarding the text against historical inquiry, but for others it provided an alternative mode of critical inquiry after the biblical materials had been stripped of these claims to historical truthfulness. This is unfortunate since it masked the capacity of Scripture to refer to "the way things really are" in terms other than historical detail. However, this misconstrual of how Scripture is true means only that we must ask anew, In what sense does Scripture refer to the truth? How do we parse its capacity to refer its readers to the way reality really is, to the way God sees what is?

Of course, as we have seen, the Bible is not devoid of historical intentions and interests, so these cannot be overlooked in our attempts to take the measure of its truth claims. As I will argue in chapter 5, however, veracity in matters of scientific detail is hardly central when the believing community comes to terms with the character of the "truth" to which Scripture points. For now, though, it is enough simply to remind ourselves that the inadequacy of in-the-text approaches to biblical interpretation lies also in their failure to take fully into account the reality to which Scripture refers.

Hence, although nothing can make up for a reader's lack of attention to "the text," in-the-text readings are increasingly viewed as important points of beginning in need of additional interpretive emphases. In fact, an interest in the text *as text* is not only an important but, indeed, an indispensable and nonnegotiable initial step.

3. *In front of the text*: Musings toward alternatives to the old, historical-critical approach to biblical studies might have been prompted long ago in the image Karl Barth made famous: the preacher with one hand clutching the Bible, the other hand clutching the newspaper. In this scenario, both the context of the reader and that of the ancient text have roles to play; the interpreter comes to the text *with interests*. Different social contexts lead to different sets of questions and different vantage points from which to ask them, and thus to different questions of the biblical texts—and thus to different (though presumably related) understandings of these texts. *Who is doing the reading?* This becomes a pivotal question, since all interpretation is influenced and conditioned by the interests and social location of the interpreter. Indeed, to push the image

beyond what Barth might have imagined, we could ask: Which news-paper does Barth's preacher have in her hand—the *New York Times* or the *Washington Times*; the *Wall Street Journal* or the *Berkeley Voice?*

At a rather abstract level, awareness of the importance of the reader in biblical studies grows out of the claim that meaning is not so much repeated or reproduced in the experience of reading; instead, reading constitutes, at least in some sense, the production of meaning. My use of the phrase "at least in some sense" comes in recognition that there is no singular perspective on the role of the reader today. Reader-oriented study is not so much a method as a constellation of approaches that share a common, basic rejection of any portrait of the reader as a mere (potential) receptacle for mean-ing. Reader-oriented approaches are scattered across a continuum according to the extent of readerly involvement they presume. Some reader-oriented approaches start from the recognition that the text manifests gaps and ambiguities that invite the participation of the reader in the production of meaning. Accordingly, although the reader has an active role to play, this is a role circumscribed by the responsibility of the reader who is to receive the text. Readers may actualize the text, but it this text that they are actualizing. Other approaches give readers more freedom, resisting restrictions on the role of the reader in the making of meaning, whether those restrictions derive from texts and their histories or from the tradi-tions of interpretation that have grown up around them. For those who champion a reading experience untroubled by outer limits, the reader has replaced the author in the historical critical paradigm as the one (solely) responsible for the generation of meaning.

The presence of plurality in readerly approaches is thus marked by differences regarding the definition of the reader and the aim of reading. Judging that texts include signals and invitations for the reader, some readers read in ways so as to be led, persuaded, and/or enlarged in their interaction with the text. Others, less sympathetic to the promptings of the text, experience reading as a process of interrogating the text, even if this entails overrunning its claims with the interests they bring to the text. The kind of reception theory I find the most compelling is exemplified by such theorists as Wolfgang Iser and Umberto Eco, each of whom, in his own way, has helped us appreciate that texts are not self-interpreting repositories of meaning insulated from outside influence.[9] For Eco, texts such as those in Scripture are characterized by the invitation for readers "to make the work" together with the author; they are rendered meaningful in personal and communal performance. Iser observes that texts are inevitably characterized by gaps that must be filled by readers; even if the text guides this "filling" process, different readers will actualize the text's clues in different ways. For both Eco and Iser, then, texts are capable of a range (though not an infinite number) of possible, valid meanings, depending on who is doing the reading, from what perspectives they read, and what reading protocols they practice.

Additionally, persons concerned with the role of the reader struggle to account for the perspective from which reading occurs.[10] That is, the question is not only what one means by "reader," but also the perspective from which the reader does the reading—and it is this awareness of "perspective" that fuels a variety of significant approaches to the hermeneutical task. For example, the historic use of the biblical materials as a tool of oppression has led to a plurality of liberationist approaches to the reading of Scripture. For those who take interpretation as nothing more than the discovery of a meaning already resident in the text, this interest in "perspective" will seem strange, just as the possibility of the Bible being used as an instrument of anything, positive or negative, may seem remote. This, however, is precisely the starting point of a liberationist hermeneutic: the recognition that all textual inquiry is shaped by the reader's context. Taking this observation seriously leads many Christians to read Scripture in fresh ways at the same time that it raises for them a fundamental critique of the commitment to observer neutrality propagated in the practice of biblical interpretation in the modern period.

By "liberationist readings," I refer to a number of interpretive strategies—for example, African American, Latino/Latina, Asian American, feminist, and womanist. Each differs from the others insofar as each arises out of its own particular history. Yet, all share some basic premises. First, no interpretation is objective, since the presuppositions, biases, and needs of readers and reading communities help determine how a text will be read. Second, each takes as its starting point a hermeneutics of suspicion, that is, a presumption of distrust at least toward traditions of interpretation, and especially traditions of interpretation arising within or nurtured among those responsible for or complicit in the colonizing of lands distant from their own, and/or for the subjugation or enslavement of persons or groups of people. After all, in many contexts, the Bible was introduced as a means of justifying colonialism and the systems of oppression that accompany it. For others, distrust reaches even further, behind the history of interpretation to the biblical texts themselves. For this latter group, even the biblical texts are the fruit of oppressive societies, and that ancient culture of oppression has placed its stamp on the pages of these texts themselves. Third, the task of engaging biblical texts does not belong primarily in the hands of academically well-trained and accredited scholars. Rather, the text belongs especially to communities of the faithful so that the only way to hear fully the message of these texts is to listen to those who live on the underside of history as they engage the Scriptures. Fourth, the goal of interpretation is the generation of dispositions and behaviors oriented toward liberation. Those who read the Bible faithfully are challenged to join in the struggle for the liberation of the oppressed.

Apart from these basic commitments, liberationist readings take many forms. This is only to be expected, given the potent relevance of context to the interpretive process. African American biblical interpretation, for example, takes its starting point from the reality that, within the context of an oppressive society, the Bible has played a formative role in assisting the survival of African Americans and their communities. Scripture has been a source of (subversive) identity and hope. The Scriptures have functioned in this way in spite of the widespread presence of interpretive practices that have not accounted for minority cultures within the dominant culture and that have failed to promote proactive responses to the liberating word of God.[11] Latino/Latina approaches to reading the Bible, however, take seriously the predominant context of Hispanics in the contemporary United States, namely, a population whose choices are often limited in social, political, and economic terms.

These forms of reading grow out of the experience of marginality, poverty, the experience of rootlessness and living as strangers in a strange land, as well as familial and interhousehold experiences that prioritize and celebrate a strong sense of solidarity and communality. From these settings, the pages of the Bible are formative of hope as Scripture interprets experienced reality as something other than "our people's lot in life," and as the Bible speaks powerfully of human worth, vocation, and peoplehood in Christ.[12]

Although our admission of the inescapable role of the reader and readerly contexts is at one level recognition of a basic anthropological reality (namely, that our interpretive work is always to some degree subjective), it raises pressing questions. If our own subjective concerns and perspectives are included in the backdrop of our interpretive work, how can it be that we will be able to find in them anything other than that for which we went looking? If reading of the Bible is decisively influenced by our cultural presuppositions, can the biblical text have any function other than that of a mirror?

To press further, I have urged that a reading of the Bible as Christian Scripture is one characterized by such dispositions as openness and willingness to be formed, by postures of receiving and hearing. How does this square with the experience of many, against whom the Bible has been wielded as a bludgeon inciting capitulation to cultural values inimical to the God who liberates Israel from bondage; the God whose scales of justice are weighted toward the alien, the orphan, and the widow; and the God whose Son proclaimed a topsy-turvy salvation: the first shall be last, and the last shall be first?

These considerations underscore the shortsightedness of reader-oriented approaches when they are practiced apart from interests that focus *in the text* and *behind the text*. The whole of the New Testament, for example, was written in the unmitigated context of empire, by and for persons whose existence was that of a minority people under imperial rule. If so much New Testament interpretation has led to an almost unquestioned support for the state, is this not because our eyes have not been able to focus on those scripts of resistance that characterize minority peoples who find ways to live among the majority while at the same time maintaining and nurturing their identity as a peculiar people? Behind-the-text considerations are capable of rescuing these texts from service as instruments of subjugation by empowering these texts to speak again with voices that arise out of the context of Roman imperial power—and which, when heard in that light, are recognized for their words of courageous resistance rather than capitulation.[13]

There are more complications. Thus, for example, I have urged that a reading of the Bible as Christian Scripture cannot be sundered from the doctrine by which the church has its identity. Accordingly, the reading community known as the church has theological constraints on what biblical texts mean. This is a central aspect of the location from which the church reads its Scriptures. Similarly, a decision to read a biblical text as a constituent of the canon of Scripture predetermines the range of possible readings of that text. Included in the range of factors comprising the location and commitments of the reader or readerly community, then, are theological factors as well as social, political, racial, and ethnic factors, factors of class, and so on.

What is the way forward? The result of these considerations is the veritable smorgasbord of methodological approaches to reading the Bible that characterizes biblical studies today—a slew of historical approaches (e.g., form, source, redaction, and tradition criticism, as well as most forms of social-scientific criticism), a handful of approaches that center on the text (e.g., older forms of narrative criticism, inductive approaches, some forms of rhetorical criticism, and the "Bible as literature" movement), and a register of approaches that account especially for the situatedness of the reader and readerly community (e.g., reader-response criticisms, feminist criticisms, Latino/Latina interpretation, African American interpretation, postcolonial criticism, and theological interpretation).[14] Some are oriented more toward locating "meaning" *behind the text*, treating the text as a window into the historical events and processes informing the text. Others accord privilege to *the text itself*, emphasizing a concern with the forms of the text or the text as literature. Still others focus on considerations *in front of the text*, accounting for (and even celebrating) the observation that different readers and readerly communities might hear a text and construe its significance differently. A newcomer to biblical studies would be forgiven for imagining that the single stable character of the discipline today is its disorderliness.

The particularly theological concerns I have outlined are relevant here, not least because they militate against the hegemonic claims of any single approach (or group of approaches). The center of the interpretive process is the text, but the text is never alone. It is itself the fruit of historical processes marinated in a concoction of sociocultural and theological interests. Reading these texts is an exercise in cross-cultural communication and understanding, and failing to appreciate this aspect of the interpretive enterprise is a recipe for the inevitable domestication of the text, guaranteeing that the voice heard in and through the text is a poor substitute for the robust, sonorous Word of God. The particularity of the text is the price of the incarnation. However, inquiry into sociohistorical factors is not an end in itself, nor is it decisive in the capacity of the believing community to discern the voice of God. Sociocultural inquiry does not give us the meaning of a text, but works to orient us to one of the contexts within which the text has significance and from which it speaks. God's intent cannot be limited by what the prophets and apostles thought they were doing when they put pen to paper, so to speak.

The particularity of biblical texts and their origins is matched, though, by the particularity of readers and their locations. We do not come naked, history-less, culture-less, objectively to the text, but bring ourselves, our formation as humans and our communities of identity, with us to the biblical text. We do so and so do others. In the negotiation of these particularities—the needs of the text and the needs of its readers—we find the significance of these texts for God's people. Given the shifting sands on which readers across time and space occupy, and given our varying grasp of the historical situatedness of the biblical texts, we are left with one stable factor in the equation of biblical interpretation. This is the text, which we embrace as Christian Scripture and so to which we allocate priority in the formation of Christian faith and life.

Again, though, these texts form the canon of Scripture, and Christians recognize in the whole of Scripture an architecture, the patterns of which guide our understanding of the significance of any of its parts. And so on.

In other words, no particular method can be identified as the correct one, nor can any method ensure a faithful reading of the Bible as Scripture. We are dealing here with a mysterious alchemy for which the biblical text serves as the single stable factor in an otherwise shifting equation. We can say, though, that any and all methods must be tamed in relation to the theological aims of Scripture and the ecclesial context within which the Bible is read as Scripture. We can also add that, for such a reading, some methods are easier to justify, are more immediately relevant, and are more theologically friendly than others. These would include approaches that regard their interpretive work as oriented toward and determined by these texts; that allow the biblical texts their role in the give-and-take of interpretation (rather than relegating them to the status of mere objects for our experimentation and inquiry), and thus situate these texts socio-historically; that account for their untamable, divine origins; that account for the theological unity of Scripture; and that account for the final form and canonical location of the biblical texts.

> **No particular method can be identified as the correct one, nor can any method ensure a faithful reading of the Bible as Scripture.**

A Close Reading of the Text
. . . in Context

From this more general exercise in mapping the terrain of method in biblical interpretation, we can move in for a more detailed examination.

In reading the Bible, *context* is critical. However, context comes in all guises, and different methods concern themselves with different understandings of context. Historical methods focus on historical context. Reader-response methods focus on the context of the reader or reading community. And so on.

One metaphor for the task of interpretation is "processing," a metaphor borrowed from the discipline of discourse analysis.[15] The utility of this image is its resistance to viewing our interpretive work as a series of steps to follow—first this, then that, and so on. Instead, reading strategies fold into one another, one set of questions inviting another in an often unruly order. Even if the image suggests the world of computer technology, processing actually resists our thinking of interpretation as a set of rules, a hermeneutical technology. This is because each reading strategy informs the others; discoveries at one point trigger reconsideration of others; the introduction of fresh insight invites reconsideration of previous study, with the result that the integrated work of interpretation is, quite literally, never done.

"Processing" is both "bottom-up" and "top-down." In bottom-up processing, we are working out the sense of words, following the sequence of a text in order to think with it by following its argument, for example, or imagining the scene it is painting. At the same time, from the top-down, we are predicting on the basis of what we are learning where the next section of the text will take us and, then, how the whole of the text is taking shape. Together, bottom-up and top-down processing engages us in an ongoing negotiation of the text's openness to fresh interpretation and the textually embedded constraints on possible construals of the text. Thinking of the task of interpretation along these lines allows a number of questions to surface. I will focus on ten areas of study, grouped with reference to their interest in establishing the text (*text*), reading the text in its literary context (*cotext*), locating the text historically and culturally (*context*), and grasping the relation of the text to other texts (*intertext*).

A Close Reading of the Text		
The Text	Textual Criticism	Through comparison of versions or the use of the original-language apparatus, have you accounted for any significant variant readings?
	Genre and Form	Have you identified "what this text is" and/or to what larger genre it belongs, and accounted for the significance of this identification?
	Determination of Boundaries	What is the smallest unit of the text that can be analyzed as a relatively self-contained unit? What markers in the text assist your analysis?
	Internal Development and Argument	Have you been able to identify the structure and/or other strategies by which the author attempts to persuade his or her audience?
	The "About-ness" of the Text	Can you (provisionally) summarize the theme of this text?

The Cotext	Situation of Text in Larger Presentation	Have you shown how your reading of this text is informed by what went on before and after?
	Important Words/Motifs	What key words and/or motifs are signaled in this text? How have you judged them to be key?
	Interpretive Possibilities	What other readings of this text are possible? What can we not know about the meaning of this text without further reading?
Context	Sociohistorical Setting	What is the setting of this text? How does our knowledge of this setting influence our reading of this text?
	Cultural Conventions/Cues	In what ways does this text depend on such taken-for-granted conventions as purity, distribution of power, social roles, honor, shame, and so forth?
	The Interface of Contexts	In what ways does this text appear to stand in tension with the world it addresses? In what ways does your own context intersect with that of this text?
Intertext	Citations and Echoes	What Old Testament passages are explicitly cited in this text? Alluded to? What is their significance in this new context?
	Intercanonical Echoes	What other passages are brought to mind by a reading of this one? What interests does this text bring to our reading of the whole of Scripture? How does a canonical perspective shed light on this text?
	Text and Creed	What interests does the creedal tradition bring to this text? What do we see in this text that we might not see apart from the prism of the classical creeds?

1. *What is the text?* Bottom-up reading starts by assuming that the biblical text before us is a given or by establishing the biblical text by means of textual criticism. This part of the interpretive process recognizes that we do not possess the original documents but only copies— copies that are not identical. Those who lack facility with the biblical languages can get some sense of potentially significant variations by comparing contemporary translations and by using a good study Bible.

2. In getting at the nature of the text, we also consider the form in which this text is presented, its genre. When we read, "First, take a cup of flour . . ." or "The elder to the beloved Gaius . . ." (3 John:1) or "With what can we compare the kingdom of God?" (Mark 4:30), certain expectations are triggered. We have before us a recognizable "form" of literature with its own "rules" for generation and "constraints" for interpretation (in these cases, a recipe, a letter, and a parable, respectively). Genre signals a tacit agreement between the writer and the reader: the writer follows certain protocols in order to invite a particular kind of reading, and the reader, acknowledging those protocols, participates in the work of reading accordingly. The writer invites the reader to a dance and the reader joins in, following the moves of the writer, we hope; were readers to imagine themselves as line dancers while the writer performs the salsa, only mishap (that is, misapprehension of the text) can result. Concern with genre is a function of top-down processing, focusing as it does on shaping readerly expectations.

3. *What is the thought unit?* Bottom-up processing identifies markers in the text denoting transitions, topic-shifts, or developments in the structure of an argument that set the boundaries of the text to

be examined. These same markers suggest the relation of a thought unit to its surrounding material—temporally (e.g., "after this," or "before sunrise"), for example, or logically (e.g., "therefore," or "because"). We recognize that the chapters and verses into which biblical texts have been divided are not original to the text and, in some cases, can be quite misleading. In the same way, how texts are broken into paragraphs, the headings supplied, the spaces in the presentation of the text—these matters of presentation are all editorial decisions made by modern translators and publishers, and are just as capable of confusing our reading as aiding it. The same can be said of lectionaries, which sometimes break a thought unit in order to trigger thematic interests that may not attend well to the text's own structure. Many of us have seen a verse ripped from its context in order to make a point, or a reading of a biblical text that stops in the middle of a sentence or paragraph since what follows does not help and might actually undermine the point the speaker wants to make.

How does the thought develop? What literary strategies does the writer use? How does the text encourage its own reading? What is the appropriate unit of textual communication for purposes of study? Usually, a thought unit is more than a verse, less than a chapter; it is a stretch of text with its own internal unity and a semblance of completeness; it is of adequate size for interpretation of its parts; and it is often set off from the material around it by genre-specific textual markers, such as changes of geography, topography, character, or time in narratives; or connectives like "therefore" or "above all," or the use of direct address in letters.

4. How is this text located in relation to the surrounding text (cotextually)? Cotext refers to the location of an utterance within a string of linguistic data, the sentences, paragraphs, and chapters surrounding and related to a text and within which it finds meaning. The importance of cotext is signaled by the ambiguity of language. Specific words are often capable of multiple meanings, giving rise to potential uncertainties whether one is reading or hearing the text read. Likewise, chunks of texts, whether phrases or sentences or even paragraphs, can be interpreted in diverse ways. Locating words in sentences, sentences in paragraphs, paragraphs in larger sections, and sections in books progressively narrows the range of possible meanings. The more cotext, the more secure the interpretation. Cotext also gets its importance from the linearity of texts: we read from left to right (in English, at least). Sentences other than the first to appear in a text have their interpretation constrained by the preceding text, as words, sentences, and entire units of discourse are shaped in their significance by the larger cotexts within which they appear. As we read, we are constantly shifting back and forth between prospective development and retrospective clarification. On the one hand, as we read we carry with us what we have just read and formulate expectations of what will follow. On the other hand, the more we read the more we are able to reconsider the significance of what has gone on before. With biblical texts, of course, our reading gives way to rereading and more rereading, so that, with each fresh encounter, we are able to grasp even more of the interpretive possibilities offered by these texts. It is no wonder, then, that we find ourselves amazed by what we have just read, even though we remember reading the same text a decade earlier.

Lack of attention to cotext is one of the more pressing problems of biblical interpretation. We read accounts in 1 Kings or the Gospel of Matthew as if they were separated from the ongoing narratives of 1 Kings or the Gospel of Matthew. Treating these accounts as individual stories, we fail to recognize how the larger narrative shapes our understanding of the one account, and, vice versa, how this single account helps shed light on the narrative as a whole. To give one example, in Luke 3:7-14, John the Baptist sketches what it would mean to be a genuine child of Abraham, in part by encouraging such "fruits worthy of repentance" as these: "Whoever has two coats must share with anyone who has none; and whoever has food must do likewise," and, for toll collectors in particular, "Collect no more than the amount prescribed for you." Is it any wonder, then, that when, sixteen chapters later, Zacchaeus reports that he gives half of his possessions to the poor and that he repays four times over those whom he has defrauded, Jesus acknowledges that salvation has come to Zacchaeus's house since "he too is a son of Abraham" (Luke 19:1-10)? Only by seeing the whole do we recognize that Zacchaeus performs "fruits worthy of repentance" according to the pattern scripted in the Gospel's opening chapters.

5. From a bottom-up perspective, issues of cotext are also concerned with how we make sense of words in the text—with regard to what words might mean and also with regard to how words might function within the text before us. Bible dictionaries or lexicons can provide us with a range of possibilities for the meaning of particular

words, but cotext is decisive in sorting through those virtual possibilities to hit upon how a term is actually used in this text.

6. *What is the setting of this text?* If we are to allow the text to speak to us as subject (rather than addressed by us as object), we will need to hear its voice from within its own cultural horizons. In day-to-day discourse with our friends and family, the work of communication can be less demanding; they share much of our base of experiences and we theirs. We can take less for granted when it comes to the folk of whom the Bible speaks. Why those clothes? Why that posture? Why that form of address? Why those concerns? A hermeneutics of hearing is first of all a hermeneutics of respect, in which we attend to the text as "other."

Because of the capacity of texts to improvise in relation to their social environments, when we attend to matters of context we may follow in the theological footsteps of the writers of biblical texts, tracing how they themselves have engaged in cultural analysis and critique. When read against the horizons of their own environments, what do these texts affirm, deny, reject, undermine, or embrace? How does this text participate in theological and ethical reflection? How does the text speak back to, against, and within its world? Work in this area enables us to hear the voice of the biblical text more clearly, rather than the voice of those who, like ventriloquists, have become skilled in controlling the text so that it speaks only as it is allowed.

7. To refer to "the setting of this text" is also to account for the setting within which this text is read, that is, our own location as readers and a readerly community. This means that we come to the

text aware of our own predilections, our own cares, our own needs, not so that we can overwhelm the text with our selves, but so that we might be open to how the text might interpret us.

8. *On what other texts does this text depend for its significance?* Every text is a node within a network of other texts, the site of multiple voices whose words take form in this new communicative setting. Other texts are "written into" this one, "entextualized," so that this text draws on the significance and power of those other texts at the same time that it reorients those earlier texts into a kind of "preferred meaning."[16] In other words, when precursor texts are removed from their former literary homes and transplanted to new ones, they bring with them the authoritative status of the old while being transformed for fresh service in the new. Their significance in their new cotext is determined primarily by that new cotext.

To attend to these voices is to recognize the role of intertextuality in interpretation of all kinds, including biblical interpretation. With ears well tuned, we can hear inner-biblical echoes within the Old Testament itself, as earlier texts are picked up and read anew in later ones. We can hear echoes of Israel's Scriptures among the New Testament writings, which seek to carry forward the story of God's engagement with God's people. We find echoes of texts and traditions from outside the Bible as well—in the case of the Old Testament, other creation or flood stories, other legal codes, or other treaties of covenant; and in the case of the New Testament, other apocalyptic writings of woe and deliverance, hints of Greco-Roman philosophical texts or religious practices, and so on. This last kind of evidence speaks to the embeddedness of biblical writings in their sociohistorical contexts, and thus serves as a prophylactic against our too easily recruiting the biblical materials to serve our interests or assessing them according to modern standards, but also serves as a boon to grasping the significance of these texts as divine self-disclosure in the particularity of the ancient world.

From the perspective of reading these texts specifically as Christian texts, the category of "other texts" of which we ought to take account expands to include (9) the whole of Christian Scripture, Old and New Testaments, and (10) the classical creeds of the Christian tradition. From a historical perspective, it is easy enough to see that Luke 4:18-19 draws on Isaiah 58:6; 61:1-2, which itself interprets the legislation regarding the Jubilee in Leviticus 25. But, within the context of the Christian canon of Scripture, other possibilities for reading emerge, so that it becomes not only possible but also necessary to read texts side by side that shared no discernible historical or traditional relationship. Whether Paul or James knew the Old Testament book of Esther, Esther is now integral to the larger canonical context within which we read Paul and James. Again, whether James wrote his letter with an awareness of Paul's apostolic mission, or whether James wrote his letter as a response to a misconstrual of Paul's message, from a canonical perspective we read them side by side as constituents of the New Testament's two letter collections, the Pauline and the general letters.

Moving further beyond the constraints of an explicit, traceable, historical lineage, the Bible is read as Christian Scripture in relation to the ecumenical creeds of the church. As I have already addressed this theological or doctrinal context for reading Scripture (see chapter 3), I will allow only a word or two of reminder to suffice. For most of the church's history, doctrine has served in a sense as the lines of the page on which to write the interpretation of Scripture. These "lines," to change the image, have provided the basic architecture for comprehending the biblical witness, the "economy" that any faithful interpretation of Scripture must bring to expression. Hence, a crucial "context" within which to read the biblical materials is the mosaic of Scripture itself, read as a single whole in its unified witness to God, its pivotal elements encapsulated in the classic creeds by which the church has determined its identity as Christian. This does not mean that the creed functions as a kind of matrix overlaying the witness of the biblical materials, so that when the biblical texts open their mouths their speech must be heard as the voice of Nicea, for example. Hopefully, enough has already been said to set aside the notion that we allow the creeds simply to overrun the biblical text. (If this were not so, would we have need for the Bible and biblical interpretation at all?) Instead, just as the earliest creedal traditions preserved already in the Old and New Testaments served to unify the people of God, orient God's people to their identity in the history of God's saving intervention, and clarify the faith of God's people in the context of its challengers, so the ecumenical creeds speak to the unity, identity, and integrity of the Christian church and its faith. Procedurally, then, we ask, When we are reading our Scriptures, what do we see through the prism of the creeds that we would not otherwise see?

Criteria for Assessing Interpretations

How do we know when we have achieved a valid interpretation of biblical texts? The answer to this question depends a great deal on the aim or aims that guide one's reading of a particular text. Persons whose primary aim is a reconstruction of the historical Jesus will have one set of criteria, for example, while those whose primary aim is to study the Christology of the Gospel of Matthew will have another. Even with this proviso, it is important to recognize that the question of validity in interpretation is the centerpoint for ongoing debate. Without rehearsing that debate,[17] I can nevertheless draw out what I take to be necessary inferences from this perspective on reading the Bible as Christian Scripture.

At the outset, however, it is important to underscore that by "valid" I do not mean "right," as if a single interpretation might exhaust the supposed singular meaning of a text. To illustrate, with reference to only one consideration, a single text might from a grammatical point of view support more than one reading, allowing, then, for a plurality (though not an unlimited range) of readings. "Cogent" and "convincing," or "supportable"—these are more apt descriptions of an interpretive process that takes seriously the potential interplay of author, text, and reader. This means that it will often be easier to determine those interpretations that are unsupportable or outside the boundaries than to authenticate or accredit another.

For readings of the Bible as Christian Scripture, how might valid interpretations be measured? An interpretation of Christian Scripture can be said to be valid when it:

- accounts for the text in its final form, without violating the language of the text (that is, its linguistic features), and without depending on a cut-and-paste job that refabricates the text in order that it might support a desirable outcome;

- accounts for the text as a whole and is consistent with the whole of the text, without violating the structural presentation of the text and without masking unfortunate aspects of the text that continue to haunt the interpreter;[18]

- accounts for the cultural embeddedness of language, allowing the text to have its voice heard in light of its sociohistorical assumptions;

- is "ruled" by its canonical embeddedness and set within the boundaries of the "rule of faith"; and

- is put into play in transformed lives lived within the community of God's people whose faith and life are determined by the Spirit of Christ.

Method or Sensibilities?

Using the term *method* when writing of biblical interpretation is risky, since "methods" are easily tied to expectations of set procedures, executable laws, robotic routines, consistent results, and repeatable outcomes. *Method* might conjure images of how-to manuals, programmable steps to take, guidelines to follow as if working on a conveyor line, or of the interpreter as a veritable meaning-making machine. Like driving a car or learning to paint, certain rules apply, but, eventually, these are internalized so that they operate at a preconscious level. Those who are beyond parroting the instructions do the best woodwork; those whose practiced hands seem almost to move on their own perform the best surgery. This is not the absence of technique as much as its enfleshment. As I have sketched it, reading the Bible as Scripture may seem painstakingly choreographed, slow, and even arduous, but is this not so at the beginning of any craft?

In a related context, Alasdair MacIntyre observes that the practice of a craft might involve procedures and steps. It might even build on a history of performance. Nevertheless, craft is ultimately defined by complexity and innovation that surpass those procedures and help constitute evolving rules.

> The authority of a master within a craft is both more and other than a matter of exemplifying the best standards so far. It is also and most importantly a matter of knowing how to go further and especially how to direct others towards going further, using what can be learned from the tradition afforded by the past to move towards the *telos* of fully perfected work. It is thus knowing how to link past and future that those with authority are able to draw upon tradition, to interpret and reinterpret it, so that its directedness towards the *telos* of that particular craft becomes apparent in new and characteristically unexpected ways.[19]

Mastering a craft thus entails developing particular intuitions, forming particular dispositions, becoming a particular kind of person whose commitments and predilections have been shaped in relation to the activity in question.

We may speak of biblical interpretation by referring to methods, but our interest is keenly directed toward the inculcation of certain sensitivities and sensibilities, the habituation of patterns, postures, and practices that express themselves as second nature, without observable calculation. Over time, our intimacy with the Christian Scriptures and the church's faith is such that we would never imagine packing our equipment in preparation for a visit to this strange land of the Bible, for it is here in the engagement with these texts that we find our true home.

Conclusion

By way of working through how we might approach our reading of biblical texts, I have borrowed a well-worn typology, dividing interpretive interests and procedures into three categories: *behind the text, in the text,* and *in front of the text.* Although a survey of biblical interpretation and interpreters would provide examples that fit comfortably in each of these columns, I have argued that the choices before us are not one versus the others, nor two versus the one. All have their role to play if we are to hear well the voice of God in these texts. At the same time, I have attempted to show why, while taking seriously the concerns and emphases of all three, priority belongs to one—the text itself.

Of course, I have added nuance to this claim. I observed that biblical texts are never complete on their own but invite readers to actualize their meaning, that texts are characterized by gaps that must be filled by readers, and that different readers will actualize the text's clues in different ways. I observed that biblical texts are never alone, but present themselves as cultural products that speak from and beyond the particularities of their origins. What is more, given the status of these texts as Scripture, their meaning is shaped by canonical and creedal contexts as well. I observed that readers are forever located and that, for a reading of the Bible as Christian Scripture, the determinative readerly context is the community of believers. With these provisos, then, I went on to urge an interpretive strategy that admitted the capacity of the text (as cultural product and as Scripture) to trump the (ecclesially located) reader in that place where "the right of the reader and the right of the text converge in an important struggle that generates the whole dynamic of interpretation."[20]

A teacher preparing her study for Sunday's class asked some time ago for my help. She was being given forty-five minutes to teach her students how to read the Bible well. What kind of answer could I give? I was stymied. Could students be outfitted with the tools of interpretation in a forty-five-minute block of time? Struggling with the question put to me, I came to realize that it placed the emphasis in the wrong place. I was asking myself, How can the church teach people to do a good job when they read the Bible? The better question, I came to realize, was, How can the church participate in forming good people so that they might read the Bible? Given the emphasis of this chapter on method, it is important to remind ourselves that possession of all of the right tools in the toolbox does not make one a carpenter or a plumber. When it comes to reading the Bible, I want a box teeming with tools, the more the better, since biblical texts present us with all sorts of challenges, and some interpretive tools are better suited than others for the challenges of a particular text. Tools, as important as they are, are never enough.

AUTHORITY

O bservant readers will recognize that, throughout the fore-going chapters, I have operated with an implicit commit-ment to the authority of Scripture, and with an implicit understanding of the nature of that authority. It is now time to make these commitments explicit by turning finally to the question of "authority." What view of authority is assumed in and cultivated by this invitation to read the Bible as Christian Scripture? Let me first orient this question from within the methodist tradition.[1]

Wesley's writings speak repeatedly to his belief in the centrality of Scripture in all matters of faith and life. Though tossed at him as words of slander, he wore such epithets as "Bible bigot," "Bible moth," and "Bible Christian" as badges of honor, and insisted that the same was true of all methodists. As Scott Jones observes in his study *John Wesley's Conception and Use of Scripture*, Wesley's own view of Scripture underscored its authority and inspiration.[2] In an earlier, more popular examination of *The Bible in the Wesleyan Heritage*, Mack Stokes claimed, "Among 'the people called

Methodists' there has never been any doubt that the Bible is the basis of Christian belief and practice."[3]

However easy it might be to affirm the centrality of Scripture within the methodist tradition, it is no simple thing to articulate how Scripture is central. This is partially because Wesley's own remarks and assertions about Scripture do not lend themselves to systematizing, and his own explicit statements concerning Scripture are not always fully on display in his actual use of Scripture.[4] Within The United Methodist Church, the problem is exacerbated by four decades of ambiguity surrounding the "Wesleyan Quadrilateral," that statement on theological method that seeks to coordinate four-fold "authorities": Scripture, Tradition, Reason, and Experience. In spite of widespread dis-ease with what many have regarded as an artificial formulation that represents neither Wesley's position and practice nor the Wesleyan tradition, the Quadrilateral is widely reputed to represent both Wesley and Wesleyan methodism, and has been embraced by other traditions as well.[5] Modern-day methodists continue to struggle with how these four "authorities" might be cor-related, and worry especially whether or how differences among them on a given topic might be adjudicated.

This is not to say that questions concerning the status of the Bible in the church are the consequence of such squabbles as these, how-ever. The roots of our dilemma run much deeper, into the cultural soil of the Enlightenment; more recently, they have found their way into the cracks and crevasses of postmodernity. In this chapter, I need to explore some historical issues in order to suggest why, today, we struggle with biblical authority. Against this backdrop, then, I want to examine how the authority of Scripture might be articulated for the church in these opening years of the third millennium.

A Tale of Three Crises

The loss of the Bible from both our public and ecclesial lives in the past half-century is not difficult to document. In an analysis of altruism and acts of compassion in the United States, published fifteen years ago, Robert Wuthnow discovered a positive relationship between charitable behavior and widespread familiarity with Jesus' parable of the good Samaritan.[6] Surely, we might think, this is evidence of the persistence of scriptural influence within our culture. What is remarkable about this "good Samaritan effect," however, is that Wuthnow found very few people who were able to recite the parable in a recognizable form and no one who actually grasped the arresting point of the story in its context in the Gospel of Luke. The same may be said for citations and allusions to the Bible in public addresses by politicians in recent years; they generally exhibit a biblical cadence or syntax but almost without fail lack the particular theological orientation of the Bible. In some cases, the words of the Bible are borrowed in order to bolster a moral mandate, but the role of Scripture in disclosing the triune God who stands behind this Word is lost. In other words, although the wisps of a biblically literate world may yet flutter around us, the actual substance and theological pattern of the Bible is largely absent.

The drama of Scripture—including creation and fall, exile and restoration, and the advent of new creation—does not shape our collective identity. This is hardly surprising in a nation whose Bill of Rights disentangles religion and official acts of government. Far more distressing is that, unfortunately, the situation is hardly any better in the church, where sermon illustrations are more likely to engage and influence if they derive from Academy-Award-winning movies than from the stories of Sarah and Abraham, much less Euodia and Syntyche. The dominant idiom of our lives in the West has become and largely remains that of the therapeutic society.[7]

This malaise with regard to the place of Scripture in the church resists facile analysis, so pervasive are its effects, so complex its etiology. At the risk of oversimplification, I want to describe it in three ways—in terms of a crisis of function, a crisis of relevance, and a crisis of authority.

1. With reference to a *crisis of function*, I want to acknowledge huge numbers of persons who explicitly embrace the authority of Scripture.[8] At the same time, I want to urge that explicit affirmations give us little traction when it comes to assessing the authoritative role of Scripture in the life of the church.

Our situation has not been greatly helped by developments within the evangelical arm of the church, especially since the early twentieth century, among whom biblical authority has come to reside particularly in the propositional content of the Bible and in affirmations concerning its trustworthiness. In the past century, American evangelicals have developed a well-nuanced vocabulary for speaking of Scripture—especially "infallibility" ("the full trustworthiness of a guide that is not deceived and does not deceive") and "inerrancy" ("the total trustworthiness of a source of information that contains no mistakes").[9] Such formulations have proved unhelpful in the use of Scripture in the life of the church. For some, this will seem an extravagant claim, so it is important for me to clarify what I am not saying. I am not urging that these affirmations are unhelpful on their own terms. It will become clear enough as I sketch a constructive proposal for scriptural authority, below, that I am not drawn to these formulations and actually regard them as incongruous with both the Wesleyan theological heritage and the nature of the Scriptures themselves, but my argument here does not depend on their utility as such. My point is more narrowly focused. I am insisting that, with regard to *the use of Scripture in the life of the church*, such affirmations do not take us very far. How can I make such a claim? My basis for doing so is threefold: Affirmations of the trustworthiness of the Bible (a) entail no guarantees regarding the faithful interpretation of Scripture, (b) extract no commitments from persons regarding fidelity to the witness of the Bible, and, in many cases, (c) are implicated in a positivism and a reductionism that find little quarter in biblical faith. In short, although scandalous, it remains true that there is no necessary path from affirmations of the trustworthiness of the Bible to reading the Bible as Christian Scripture.

Let me take the first two claims, (a) and (b), together. If, as I have urged, the authority of Scripture is best discerned in the lives (and not only the assertions) of those communities oriented around Scripture, then affirmations regarding Scripture are never enough. I regard this conclusion as self-evident, but will illustrate it with ancient and contemporary examples. On the one hand, this truism is on display in the Gospels and Acts, where "the battle for the Bible" focuses not on *whether* the Scriptures of Israel are to be taken seriously, but on *how* those Scriptures are to be understood within the framework of God's purpose and appropriated within the lives of God's people. Pharisees have one view of how to read the ongoing agenda of God in the Scriptures, the Jewish elite residing in Jerusalem have another view, and Jesus has still another—all with regard to the same authoritative Scriptures. This is not a struggle over how best to construe biblical authority; rather, it is a hermeneutical quandary—and one with such high stakes that differences of viewpoint surrounding the message of these Scriptures would lead eventually to the execution of one of its interpreters, Jesus. On the other hand, a more contemporary example is the Jehovah's Witnesses, who affirm biblical inerrancy and promote its literal interpretation. This is a viewpoint that, however admirable, still does not bring the theological commitments of the Jehovah's Witnesses into line with the Christian faith as this is articulated either in the ecumenical creeds of the Christian church (or even a modern ecumenical organization such as the National Council of Churches) or in the often more specific doctrinal affirmations developed among Christian denominations since.

What of my third claim (c), that affirmations of the trustworthiness of the Bible are implicated in a positivism and a reductionism that deserve little quarter in biblical faith? By placing the two terms *positivism* and *reductionism* side by side, I am referring to a tendency to reduce the witness of Scripture to its propositional content and scriptural "truth" to what can be verified through observable data.

This is the view that we can translate the ancient message of the Bible into its basic ideas, for retranslation into contemporary idiom in order to set out what the Bible says about God, humanity, and the cosmos. The difficulties here are several. One has to do with the nature of the language and thought forms comprising the biblical materials. For example, the biblical witness embraces a complex and dynamic interaction of different sorts of language and modes of expression, including analogy, poetry, narrative, legislation, performative utterances, epistle, apocalyptic, parable, and more. How does one summarize the basic idea of a poem or a narrative or an account within a narrative? Certainly, we can add an interpretive gloss ("This poem is about . . ."), but this is hardly the same thing as grasping (and being grasped by) its meaning. I have often heard the story, "Jesus washed the disciples' feet" (John 13:1-20), boiled down to an object lesson on "service"—a handy way to ward off the extremist perspectives on the dispositions and practices of interpersonal leadership and relationality inherent in Jesus' words, "If I, your Lord and Teacher, have washed your feet, you also ought to wash one another's feet. For I have set you an example, that you also should do as I have done to you" (John 13:14-15). And what definition of "truth" can be used to deduce whether a parable or oracle or poem, and any of several others constitutive of this variety of linguistic expressions, is "true"? True with respect to what?

In fact, typically, persons occupying a neutral ledge on which to adjudicate such matters do not make claims to truth and trustworthiness in reference to Scripture.[10] Instead, these are theological judgments. This does not diminish their significance, but only acknowledges that our judgments in these matters arise within a tradition. Nor in making such a claim am I sounding a retreat into postmodern perspectivalism. I am not denying that the way the biblical materials portray things is "as they actually are," but rather admitting that our capacity to see this "reality" is not a natural capacity we share but a divine gift nurtured within a particular community of interpretation. This is the church, which comes to Scripture to learn what God has said and is saying about humanity and the cosmos; it is there, in the community of the faithful, that we have our ears and eyes restored so as to hear and see, from God's perspective, "what actually is." Whether one believes that Jesus Christ is (or is not) the self-disclosure of God will have a determinative role in the credence one allows the biblical witness both to Jesus and to the God who raised him from the dead. Whether we see the truth depends on our commitments and on whether we do the truth, on whether we present ourselves to God in willingness to be transformed (cf. John 7:17; Rom. 12:1-2).[11] In fact, arguments in favor of the special status of the Bible, that is, the Bible as Christian Scripture, tend to convince those who need little convincing: those who are already inclined to grant (perhaps are even practiced in granting) the Bible this status. This is not surprising given that theological arguments are themselves best characterized as "faith seeking understanding."

The difficulty here is that modern persons who think of themselves as Christians and who identify themselves with the Christian church have often been enculturated to imagine not only that they *can* but indeed that they *must* approach the Scriptures dispassionately.

And this leads to the sense that in order for the Bible to be true it must be objectively true. But how is this possible? In raising this question, I am acknowledging the profound influence of René Descartes (1596–1650) on modern perspectives on the Bible and in modern biblical studies. His perception of knowledge in terms of a mind grasping a subject has led to a traditional image of interpretation along these lines: the objective interpreter finds the meaning already inherent in the thing being interpreted. Many modern methods of biblical interpretation, then, were engineered to analyze the text with the aim of extracting from it the intention of its author, that is, the meaning that the author placed in the textual container created by the author. Similarly, many modern views of biblical authority have maintained that the truth of the Bible is or ought to be evident to any dispassionate observer. This view is no longer tenable.

In order to return to my focus on our understanding of the authority of Scripture and its truthfulness from within a tradition, let me make two remarks—the first, briefly, in the area of hermeneutics, and the second an illustration from the New Testament and early Christianity.

The hermeneutical road from Descartes forward is lengthy and winding, and I do not plan to trace it here. Instead, in order to suggest something of the terms of the debate, I want to draw attention to some of its key milestones by summarizing four perspectives. For his part, Hans-Georg Gadamer urged that the "scientific method" (to which biblical studies has long been beholden) is not the only way to truth, proposing in its stead an even more basic category of hermeneutical reflection. In his formulation, art, for example, is "known" through a hermeneutical "game" in which we are transformed in relation to it. With regard to texts, Gadamer analogously calls for a type of hermeneutical consciousness whereby the act of understanding is imagined as a fusion of one's own horizon (that is, confronting one's own historicality) with the historical horizon embodied in these texts from the past. Objecting to this apparent relativizing of meaning, E. D. Hirsch attempted to show that one could speak of the timeless validity of a fixed interpretation. Differences in how people read texts, for Hirsch, are the result of their finding the "significance" for their context of the single "meaning" of a text, which he identified with the intent of the author. Among attempts to mediate between these poles, the work of Paul Ricoeur is paramount. Prioritizing neither the preunderstandings of the reader nor a fixed textual meaning, he emphasizes interpretation as putting the text into play, that is, appropriation of a text is focused in the text's refiguration of the reader. Finally, in an interesting transformation of Hirsch's concern with authorial intent with respect to the Bible, Kevin Vanhoozer has recently insisted on the priority of authorial intent, though while naming God as the author of the Bible. This allows him to speak of textual meaning in the singular without denying multiple readings of the same text. In the same way that the four Gospels are four interpretations of the one gospel, the one event of Jesus Christ, so there can be multiple interpretations of the one text. The one true interpretation of the text is best approximated by a diversity of readings since no one culture or mode of interpretation is adequate to exhaust its one meaning, which is the Word, the divine self-disclosure in Christ.[12] Of course, Vanhoozer's contribution to the discussion (unlike the others) is explicitly Christian, and so presumes a theological location for readers of the Bible. Though from a variety of perspectives, it nonetheless emerges that the stable factor in the alchemy of interpretation is the text, but, rather than grasping the text "as it really is," we construe texts always in relationship to the person engaged in the process of reading. The person whose patterns of thought, feeling, belief, and behavior reflect (or are beginning to reflect) a commitment to the Bible as Scripture, then, will read those pages through a different set of lenses—one, we must say, that is far more congruent with the divine aim disclosed in and through Scripture than would otherwise be possible.

I promised an example of the importance of interpretive context. Consider, then, that central event for Christian faith and practice, the crucifixion of Jesus of Nazareth. Of all that we can know of Jesus, this is the single most certain historical datum—reported, as it is, in Jewish, Roman, and Christian sources. Here, we may argue, is an objective truth to which Scripture points: the execution of Jesus on a Roman cross. Yet, the objective reality of Jesus' death on a Roman cross is a fact of little interest to anyone, Christian or otherwise, apart from (a) the theological claim that the manner of Jesus' death is interwoven with the narrative of his life, a claim that is front and center in the New Testament Gospels; and (b) the further theological claim that his execution was the death of Christ "for us," a claim that pervades the New Testament writings.[13] In other words, the "truth" that we most need is not that which can be proved in a science laboratory through repeatable experiments or multiple accounts, but *a view of life and the cosmos as it really is from God's perspective.* In this example, how a Roman historian, an opponent of the Christian movement, and a follower of Christ each viewed the same event, Jesus' death on a cross, would represent a different view of what actually was taking place. For the Christian, this "actuality" includes the salvific work of God—a perspective that is not historically verifiable but that nonetheless accounts for what "is." In this ultimate sense, then, the Bible does not "contain" the objective truth. Instead, the Scriptures refer to that truth, namely, the life of the triune God. The difficulty for traditional ideas of the objective authority of the Bible, of course, is that no one—that is, those who are not already on the journey of faith by means of the prevenient grace of God—is likely to admit this truth apart from the quickening of the Holy Spirit.

2. What of the *crisis of relevance?* To the rank and file of the church, one of the most puzzling aspects of modern study of the Bible is surely the degree to which academic biblical studies is unrelated to, often uninterested in, the venture of speaking of God. Since the eighteenth century the reigning paradigm in biblical studies has been focused on isolating matters of description (What does the Bible say?) from matters of prescription (Who should we be, and what should we believe and do in light of the biblical witness?). Thus, biblical study has become a specialization open only to those capable of handling these texts according to scholarly procedures. Issues of religious significance have consistently been marginalized from concerns of biblical interpretation. Biblical study, identified above all as historical study of the

Bible, has defined the truth of the biblical material primarily in terms of historical veracity, and repeatedly answered with profound skepticism. Historical study of the Bible has emphasized the altogether alien character of the world of the Bible, digging more deeply and widely the chasm separating us from the biblical message. As a consequence of these currents in biblical studies, many graduates from our theological institutions (across the theological spectrum) must look elsewhere for a word to proclaim. That is, faced with the task of preparing a sermon on a passage from Daniel or Matthew, the preacher dutifully consults the major critical commentaries, discovers plentiful historical and philological data and assessment of scholarly views, but is generally confronted with little help indeed for the risky business of speaking of God here and now on the basis of this text.

One of the most astonishing ironies about these developments is that it was Karl Barth made popular the phrase "the strange new world within the Bible." In a lecture delivered in 1916, he asks, "What sort of country is spread before our eyes when we throw the Bible open?"[14] Biblical studies—whether among scholars, in undergraduate or seminary classrooms, or in many local churches—would today answer this question with regard to historical strangeness: they spoke a different language, they wore different clothes, they had different forms of economic exchange, they had different ritual practices, they had different assumptions about relationships, and on the list would go. Here is the irony. For Barth, the answer was this: "within the Bible there is a strange, new world, the world of God." He continues by insisting that the "stuff" of the Bible is not fundamentally about human history, human thoughts, and human practices.

The Bible tells us not how we should talk with God but what he says to us; not how we find the way to him, but how he has sought and found the way to us; not the right relation in which we must place ourselves to him, but the covenant which he has made with all who are Abraham's spiritual children and which he has sealed once and for all in Jesus Christ. It is this which is within the Bible. The word of God is within the Bible. . . . We have found in the Bible a new world, God, God's sovereignty, God's glory, God's incomprehensible love.[15]

The astonishing thing, then, is that Barth's *theological* notion of the Bible's "strange world" could so easily and pervasively be morphed into a *historical* definition of the Bible's strangeness.

Someone may urge that, irrespective of Barth's emphases, the church must account for the historical gulf separating our world from the biblical world, and, indeed, that my own reflections on method in chapter 4 likewise assert the necessity of overcoming the historical distance of the biblical materials. This, however, would be erroneously and unnecessarily to equate "otherness" with "distance." I have insisted that, in order to allow the biblical materials to address us as Scripture, we cannot neglect the incarnationality of Scripture; they embody God's word in another time and place. I have insisted that, in order to allow Scripture its capacity as subject to address us, we cannot overwhelm it with our egocentrisms and ethnocentrisms, but instead must accept that we are engaged in intercultural discourse. That is, the Bible, when granted the status and role of Christian Scripture, is not an object to be examined or an extension of our own personalities or a container of the cultural presuppositions that I and people like me share. Scripture is subject (in the sense of its performative capacity to speak to and shape us) and other (in the sense of situating itself as partner in discourse). And this is a very different view of the biblical materials than the view inherent in attempts to discover what the text said back there and then.

In short, the practical effect of widespread and long-held commitments in the area of biblical interpretation has been to undermine the centrality and authority of the Bible. How? By promoting approaches to Bible reading that have to do with our mastering its data, rather than our being mastered by its message; by bypassing the theological claim of Scripture to speak truthfully of the transforming light that shines in the darkness and that the darkness has not overcome; by turning a blind eye to the theological claim of Scripture to recount a single narrative, from creation to new creation; and by failing to heed the invitation of Scripture to inhabit that narrative as the people of God addressed in its pages. Accordingly, what possible relevance might these texts have for us?

> **We must not promote approaches to Bible reading that have more to do with our mastering its data than with our being mastered by its message.**

3. Finally, I refer more generally to a *crisis of authority*. The impediments we face when fashioning a coherent and useful understanding of the role of Scripture in the church are tied to more pervasive cultural movements represented succinctly in the famous bumper sticker that reads, "Question Authority!" That is, the difficulty we

face today when speaking of biblical authority is intimately related to a more overarching aversion to authority as such. We may recall from chapter 3 the work of Charles Taylor, whose explorations into the making of the modern "self" found that personal identity has come to be based on presumed affirmations of the human subject as autonomous, disengaged, self-sufficient, and self-engaged. From these presumptions flow a personal identity characterized by self-sufficiency, self-legislation, self-determination, and self-autonomy.[16]

To add further to this portrait we might recall the classic account of the American middle class, *Habits of the Heart*. In that study, Robert Bellah and his research team identified "autonomous individualism" as the defining quality of American life, with concomitant emphases on "finding yourself," gaining independence, "pulling myself up by my own bootstraps"—or, as they put it, by freedom through mobility and detachment from social obligation.[17] Of course, Bellah's study was immediately critiqued for giving insufficient attention to minority traditions within the United States—African American and Hispanic-American communities, for example, as well as the potential influence of feminism.[18] As well aimed as such criticisms might be, we should not overlook the fragmentation of even minority communities as they extend their longevity among the dominant culture of the United States.[19] What of new emphases on community alleged to have arisen with postmodernism? This "new" orientation to community deserves closer scrutiny, too. As Robert Wuthnow has recognized, these new expressions of "community" are characterized more by their breadth than their depth. This brand of "community" places few demands on its "members," who are more likely to control their sense and experience of community than to subject themselves to the commitments and obligations tied to such relationships. Movement from friend to friend, group to group, or church to church comes with relative ease in the service of a self-service, do-it-yourself "community life."[20] In other words, in spite of cultural diversity within the United States and even in the face of evolving aspects of the majority culture, human identity is still implicated in emphases of autonomy and self-legislation.

For readers of Scripture, of course, these philosophical and sociological observations, however distasteful they might be in their attempts to have us look at our own reflections in the mirror, hold no surprises. Most of us need little guidance in recognizing that, as a human family, we are some distance from biblical notions of personal identity ineluctably nested in social relationships, biblical emphases on relational interdependence for human life and identity, and the premium placed by Scripture on the health and integrity of the human community.[21] For this, we need look no further than Genesis 3, which, though it introduces no particular vocabulary of sin (such as "disobedience" or "doing evil"), provides no less a profound conception of sin. According to Old Testament theologian H. D. Preuss, in Genesis 3 sin is "understood as the failure to recognize the authority of God . . . as preferring to discuss the divine word rather than observe it." Such behavior is the denial of human responsibility to God, the willful attempt for humans to make themselves lord of their own lives.[22]

If we have found it increasingly difficult to posit as an authority anything external to ourselves, if "growing up" has conventionally been tied to achieving independence and autonomy, then we may not be surprised to discover that attempts to express the authority of the Bible have largely fallen on hard times. The church may not be "of the world," but its contemporary views of and practices with reference to the Bible and its authority have very much been shaped on the potter's wheel of the modern world.

Renewing Biblical Authority

That we should speak of the need and possibility of the renewal of the place of Scripture in the life of the church is also a sign of the times. I have urged that the roots of much of our current dilemma have drawn their nourishment from assumptions and commitments characteristic of the modern age. One of the primary characteristics of modernity has been its troublesome relation to history. If, as people in the West have understood in the last three centuries, all knowledge is historically grounded, then we moderns should not be governed by someone else's history—not by the history of the Christian tradition, and not by the history of God's people related in the Bible. Moreover, the Bible has its own history and it is only within the horizons of its history that the Bible has meaning; hence, the Bible has no necessary relevance for people in other times and places. Meaning belongs "back there." Even those who thankfully rejected this view of things have not necessarily escaped its manacles. More often than not, conservative students of Scripture, too, have worked "back there" at locating the text's "original meaning," and in doing so ignored the perspectives of contemporary interpreters; neglected the theological claim that the history of these biblical texts is, in a profound sense, our history; and disregarded the traditions of the church informing (in countless ways, both formally and informally) our readings of the texts. Modernity has nurtured practices of biblical interpretation oriented toward pinning down the meaning of a biblical text, deciphering it once-and-for-all, mastering and controlling it.

The answer to our dilemma is hardly the embrace of postmodernity, for it has the propensity to discard history altogether, and with it all notions of authoritative history.

What is needed, instead, are new possibilities for thinking not *against* history (as in the modern period) but *with* history. That is, we need to recover the freedom to engage with ancient texts as our texts, and with respect and expectancy, as those who thus might embrace Scripture's theological vision and be molded according to its patterns of faith and life.

> **We need to recover the freedom to engage with ancient texts as our texts, and with respect and expectancy, as those who thus might embrace Scripture's theological vision and be molded according to its patterns of faith and life.**

What fresh visions of biblical authority are open to us today? I want to suggest that we think of biblical authority in terms of (1) the Bible's intrinsic authority, (2) the authority of the biblical narrative, (3) biblical authority as invitation, and (4) biblical authority as grace.

1. *The Intrinsic Authority of the Bible*: One of the hallmarks of talk of scriptural authority in the past two centuries has been the degree to which it has been given over to making claims on the Bible's behalf. Unfortunately, it has done so, typically, in idiom that is foreign to the biblical witness itself. Claims regarding the Bible's "truthfulness," for example, beg the question, Whose truth? It is easy enough to answer, "God's truth!" without taking seriously enough that the actual canons of truth against which the Bible was to be measured have been those of the emerging rationalism and the scientific method. Within the Wesleyan tradition, we find a profound alternative. Recall the words from Wesley's preface to his *Sermons on Several Occasions*:

> I want to know one thing, the way to heaven,—how to land safe on that happy shore. God himself has condescended to teach the way: for this very end he came from heaven. He hath written it down in a book. . . . I read his Book; for this end, to find the way to heaven.[23]

Given this affirmation, we might insist that Wesley's own view of the Bible's truthfulness would not find its true test in its historicity or the conformity of its words and phrases to the ever-expanding claims of the natural sciences. Rather, this test of its truthfulness would rest on whether Scripture does, indeed, allow me "to know one thing, the way to heaven,—how to land safe on that happy shore."

How does the Bible assert its own authority? In fact, it does so only rarely, and this presses us to make a key distinction between two sorts of authority: extrinsic and intrinsic. The first sort of authoritative statement, the extrinsic one, we accept as true not because the statement itself is compelling but because we grant the speaker the authoritative status necessary to make that statement. However, if the statement itself is convincing or compelling, irrespective of who said it, then we might say that we recognize its intrinsic authority. Most Christians relate to the Bible by granting it some combination of intrinsic and extrinsic authority. Scripture itself presents its appeal in a variety of ways—calling upon our imaginations, reminding us of our commitments, asking us to consider reasoned arguments, urging us to engage in self-reflection on our experience as God's people—persuading and convincing, but rarely demanding. As John Goldingay helpfully summarizes, "Scripture as a whole is more inclined to seek to persuade us of the truth of things than to expect us to 'believe seven impossible things before breakfast.'"[24]

In the end, that famous example of deduction—"God says it; I believe it; that settles it"—does not represent very well the Bible's own way of speaking of itself. Instead, we find that as we give ourselves to the life of the Spirit and engagement with Scripture, God so works in our lives and imaginations that we are led further into the biblical narrative, so that we find the

> **What is needed most are people deeply embedded in faithful communities of discipleship, people in whom the Spirit is actualizing the Word of God and, thus, for whom the Word of God is authenticated.**

Bible more and more to be true. This means, as I have already urged, that those of us who seek after methods for reading and interpreting the Bible correctly are usually looking for the wrong thing. What is needed most are people deeply embedded in faithful communities of discipleship, people in whom the Spirit is actualizing the Word of God and, thus, for whom the Word of God is authenticated.

2. *The Authority of the Biblical Narrative*: One of the difficulties with the way biblical authority has been articulated in the past century has been its focus on the truth of Scripture's propositions. This is problematic because, far and away, the majority of Scripture does not assert in prose but narrates. The bulk of Scripture is narrative, so it is worth inquiring into the sort of truth-claims made by biblical narrative.

The category of "narrative" when applied to the biblical materials may seem strange to some, but the impetus for engaging Scripture and its message in these terms comes from Scripture itself. This is true, first, in that the bulk of Scripture comes to us in the form of narratives. Although theology in the modern period has gravitated toward the rational essence of the faith, its dogmatic essentials, scriptural reflections on God's nature have a different flavor. Rather than enumerating the immutable attributes of God, the Bible has it that

> God's person emerges in a series of contexts. God is a creator, then a destroyer. God relates to a family in the concerns of its ongoing family life, such as the finding of a home, the birth of children, and the arranging of marriages; God then relates to a nation in the different demands of its life, which includes God's becoming a war-maker. . . . The "revelation" of God's person is inextricably tied to the events in which God becomes different things, in a way that any person does; it is thus inextricably tied to narrative. [25]

Moreover, we find in biblical texts the deliberate work of forming God's people by shaping their story. Israel's first "credo" took the form of a narrative: "A wandering Aramean was my ancestor" (Deut. 26:5-10). The speeches in Acts interpretively render the history of Israel so as to demonstrate the advent of Jesus as its culmination (e.g., Acts 7:2-53; 13:16-41). And John's Revelation portrays the whole of history from creation to new creation so as to transform the theological imagination of its readers.[26] Finally, the particular narratives related in the biblical books, together with the nonnarrative portions of Scripture, participate in a more extensive, overarching narrative (or metanarrative). This is the story of God's purpose coming to fruition in the whole of God's history with us—from the creation of the world and humanity's falling away from God, through God's repeated attempts to restore his people, culminating in the coming of Jesus of Nazareth, and reaching its full crescendo in the final revelation of Christ and the new creation. In an important sense, the Bible is nothing less than the record of the actualization (and ongoing promise) of this purpose of God in the history of the cosmos.

Does biblical narrative promise to tell us "what actually happened," so that we may measure its truthfulness by its verisimilitude and arbitrate its authority by proving that "things happened as the Bible reports them"? We cannot escape the sense that historical analysis in biblical studies has been and is characterized by its inhospitality toward concerns with narrativity. For example, in a fascinating example of doublespeak, New Testament scholar Philip Esler observes, on the one hand, that "Christianity is a religion of a series of revelatory acts to which certain texts bear witness in a manner which has subsequently been settled as authoritative,"[27] and, on the other hand, that social-scientific exegesis can help us excise distortions of "the bedrock of our tradition" that have crept into that story.[28] This example highlights the basic problem with narrative and narrative theology for many, namely, the commitment of the historical critic to the methodological priority of discovering firm bedrock in the history behind the text as the foundation on which to build the message of the church. In the two statements above, this commitment stands in tension with Esler's recognition of authoritative texts. In a related vein, in a massive study, *Jesus Remembered*, James Dunn locates his discussion of narrative study of the Gospels in a chapter entitled "The Flight from History."[29]

On account of the different concerns of historical-critical study and narrative approaches, an unfortunate choice has often been forced upon students of narrative: historicity or creativity. Indeed, the influence of the Yale school (as represented above all by George Lindbeck) in narrative study has led to a wholesale concern regarding the alleged indifference of narrative theology to the historicity of the biblical story—whether externally referential events comprise the biblical narrative.[30] This, of course, is not a problem solely for Lindbeck or biblical narrative in particular, but has been endemic to discourse on the narrative representation of historical events more generally in the last half of the twentieth century.[31] Whether fictional or historical, what mattered most has often seemed to be the "meaning" provided within and by narrative.

However, more recent work in the philosophy of history has urged that "narrative" need not be so much *creation* of significance through the imposition of interpretive frameworks, but rather the *recognition* of thematic and causal ties among events in the real world.[32] Clearly, there are ways of accounting for the relation of narrative to its external referents other than by denying the creative and critical acumen of the narrator. As James Phelan has written in his study *Narrative as Rhetoric*: "That our facts change as our narrative frameworks change does not prove that there are no facts; it proves rather than there are multiple facts and multiple ways of construing facts."[33] Maturing perspectives on the nature of narrative, then, have rendered problematic facile claims concerning the disinterest in or rejection of historical questions in narrative study.

This is not to deny the need for historical investigation, of course. If the biblical materials purport to narrate human-divine relations, then the Bible itself invites historical questions, not least of such key events as God's deliverance of Israel from Egypt and the advent of Jesus of Nazareth. Having said this, however, it is important to realize that historical study could never *prove* the incarnation, for example, in the sense of demonstrating that Jesus was God-in-the-flesh. Historical study can and should explore the evidence for Jesus, together with the cultural conditions within which he lived, conducted his ministry, and was executed. Historical study can and should explore the evidence for the Christian claim that Jesus was raised from the dead. But historical study cannot on its own speak to such questions as whether Jesus is God's Son, whether Jesus was the long-awaited Messiah, whether Jesus died for our sins, or whether Jesus' resurrection signaled the restoration of God's people and the ushering in of the new age.

Hence, the line that separates emphases on narrative and history should not be drawn with regard to their relative interests in historical events and historical veracity. Instead, narrative studies will be segregated from historical inquiry by the former's essential concern with the subjective engagement of its audience, its invitation to its audience to live in the new world it proposes. Narrative is less about chronicling events and more about drawing out their significance and inviting response. To put it differently, "narrative" is not just "story" but also "action." Indeed, narration is a particular telling of a story to a particular audience in a particular situation in order to achieve a particular end.[34] Narrative, then, is an exercise in influence.

Hence, the first questions narrative invites are not about historical veracity ("Did this really happen this way?"), but about signification ("What does this mean?") and invitation ("What does this call me to be and do?"). This is not to say that these narratives are lacking in historical referents; it is to say that the interpretive task is not satisfied by questions of historicity, but rather by questions of meaning, aim, purpose, signification.

The truth-claim made by biblical narrative, then, lies above all in the claim of narrative to speak, as it were, on God's behalf. These narratives present themselves in their capacity to interpret reality in light of God's self-disclosure of God's own character. Here we find the will of God working itself out in the cosmos and on the plain of human events. In this sense, the Bible's authority as Christian Scripture rests in its status as *revealed history*.

> **The Bible's authority rests, ultimately, in its disclosure of this divine purpose.**

This has significance for our reading of individual narratives, say, 1 Samuel or the Gospel of Mark. At a more profound level, though, "revealed history" is characteristic of the whole of the biblical witness, with the canon of Scripture understood as witness to a single narrative that extends from creation to new creation. It is too much to say that this narrative is "contained" within the Bible, since the biblical materials both recall God's work before the establishment of the cosmos and anticipate the consummation of God's purpose at the End and beyond. Nevertheless, the plotline is very much set within its pages. That is, there is no making sense of what God is doing in the world apart from tracing the line of his purpose from creation, through his mighty acts of redemption in Exodus and the advent of Jesus Christ, and on to the restoration of all things. It is in light of this beginning, middle, and end that all else finds it meaning. This itself is a reminder *both* that events take their meaning from the narrative as a whole *and* that, like narratives more generally, the biblical narrative moves forward in the service of a central aim, in relation to which all else is oriented. In this important sense, the Bible is not really "about" humanity; nor is it a christological book, in the narrow sense. Rather, its plot is *theo*logically determined; its subject and center is God, infleshed in Jesus Christ, active powerfully and formatively through Word and Spirit. Yahweh's purpose thus determines the shape of this narrative and issues to its readers the invitation to read themselves into this ongoing narrative and thus to choose sides, that is, to align their lives around the overarching purpose of God. The Bible's authority rests, ultimately, in its disclosure of this divine purpose.

3. *Biblical Authority as Invitation:* It is never enough to make affirmations about the authority of Scripture. This is because what it means to refer to the Bible as Christian Scripture is to declare its role in shaping a people, transforming their most basic commitments, their dispositions, and their identities. The *narrative of Scripture* is a unitary story about the world—not only the world of the past, but the world we inhabit. Hence, "to be a Christian is in some sense to have one's own story shaped in a decisive way by and taken up into this other larger story of God's redemptive action in the world."[35] Theologian Trevor Hart writes:

> It is precisely here that moral conviction of the truth of this story, and hence its authority, is rooted. God speaks. He convinces us that things between himself and the human race are in reality much as they are in the story. We are drawn into the world of the text precisely as we are drawn into a relationship with its central character [that is, with God]. As this happens, we find ourselves confronted by many of the same realities and experiences as are narrated in the text. Suddenly, sin, guilt, grace, reconciliation, the power of God's Spirit, the risen Christ and so on are not mere elements in a narrative world, but constituent part of our own world, players and factors to be taken into consideration in our daily living and our attempts to make sense of our own situation.[36]

In short, the authority of Scripture is less demand and more invitation to come and live this story, to inhabit the narrative of God's ongoing and gracious purpose for his people. The authority of Scripture is an invitation to resist attempts at revising the words of

Scripture so as to make them match our reality and instead is an invitation to make sense of our reality, our lives, within its pages, according to its story. To embrace the Bible as Christian Scripture, then, is to accept it not as one narrative among others, but to accord it a privilege above all others, and to allow ourselves to be shaped by it ultimately.

4. *Biblical Authority as Grace:* The narrative that is Scripture does not first require assent, then, but invites and, indeed, draws us into its world. It engages us imaginatively as we follow its path through the lives of our traveling companions: Seth and Enoch, Joseph and Ruth, Sarah and Daniel, Martha and Priscilla. Precisely because Scripture is first and foremost about God, it draws its chief character from God. How, then, could the authority of Scripture be anything but a gracious gift, an expression of divine care? If the gracious character of God grounds divine-human relations in God's generous initiative and sustaining faithfulness, culminating in the powerful, restorative activity of God on behalf of humanity, then the claims of Scripture on our lives could never be mistaken for expressions of coercive power or a kind of divine "trump card" held by God (or by God's agents) to be played when backed into a corner. On the night of his betrayal, Jesus submits to God's will, not as one lacking backbone, kneeling before an authoritarian command, but as one who discerns God's purpose and embraces it as his own (Luke 22:39-46). This is not to deny that obedience sometimes comes before understanding; the story of Abraham, whether one thinks of his initial call from God to "go . . . to the land that I will show you" (Gen. 12:1) or to offer his own son as sacrifice (Gen. 22:1-14), is evidence

enough of the priority of faith. Even these events must be located within the wider narrative of Scripture, however, and thus set within the wider self-disclosure of God, for whom outward appearances are hardly the measure of reality (see Hab. 3:17-18). Theology, after all, even a theology of Scripture, is faith seeking understanding.

Conclusion

Reading the Bible as revealed history entails asking how these events, these stories, fit within the grand story of God's creation and redemption. It means taking seriously the implicit claim of historical narratives within the Bible to provide God's perspective on what historical events are most important, and why they are important. This does not entail our reading the Bible in ways that open a great chasm between biblical times and our own. The strangeness of the Bible resides in the strangeness of God's gracious and salvific character and purpose when compared with the goings-on that typify our world. But this is a strangeness that invites rather than repels.

We participate in the grand story of God's work too. As we read the Bible as revealed history, we come better to understand that this story is our story. We come to understand the events and progress of our own lives within the perspective of the narrative of Scripture.

Reading the Bible as Christian Scripture entails an explicitly Christian position, one that affirms that the Old and New Testaments are inseparable in their witness to God the Savior and that the coming of Christ is the point of orientation that gives all biblical books their meaning as Scripture. Even if Christians have long pushed the Old Testament to the margins, the reality is that we cannot know Jesus Christ genuinely apart from the God of Jesus Christ revealed first in the Scriptures of Israel.

Even though we recognize that each book of the Bible was written to people and in places far removed from us in time and culture, when we approach the Bible as Christian Scripture we take seriously the faith statement that this book is our Book, these scriptures are our Scripture. We are not reading someone else's mail—as though reading the Bible had above all to do with recovering an ancient meaning intended for someone else and then translating its principles for use in our own lives. When we recall that *we* are the people of God to whom the Bible is addressed as Scripture, we realize that the decisive transformation that must take place is not the transformation of an ancient message into a contemporary meaning, but rather the transformation of our lives in terms and by means of God's Word.

> **We come not so much to retrieve facts or to gain information, but to be formed.**

Accordingly, reading the Bible as Scripture has especially to do with our dispositions as we come to our engagement with Scripture. We come not so much to retrieve facts or to gain information, but to be formed. The Bible's authority rests, ultimately, in its disclosure of this divine purpose.

NOTES

1. Reading the Bible, Reading Scripture

1. Wesley A. Kort, *"Take, Read": Scripture, Textuality, and Cultural Practice* (University Park: Penn State University Press, 1996), 1.

2. "The Bible and Public Schools: A First Amendment Guide" (Nashville: First Amendment Center, 1999), 5. The Society of Biblical Literature Council added its name to the list of organizations endorsing the statement on April 29, 2006.

3. See Robert Wuthnow, *Sharing the Journey: Support Groups and America's Quest for Community* (New York: Free Press, 1994).

4. Robert J. Sternberg, "It's Not What You Know, But How You Use It: Teaching for Wisdom," *Chronicle of Higher Education*, June 28, 2002, B20.

5. Robert Morgan with John Barton, *Biblical Interpretation* (Oxford: Oxford University Press, 1988), 15; see pp. 1-43.

6. David Kelsey, *The Uses of Scripture in Recent Theology* (Philadelphia: Fortress Press, 1975), 90.

7. Cf. Kort, *"Take, Read,"* 2-3; John Webster, *Holy Scripture: A Dogmatic Sketch* (Cambridge: Cambridge University Press, 2003).

8. Wuthnow, *Sharing the Journey*, 245.

9. For estimates related to letter production, see E. Randolph Richards, *Paul and First-century Letter Writing: Secretaries, Composition and Collection* (Downers Grove, IL: InterVarsity Press, 2004), 156-70. I refer to the Letter to the Galatians as "relatively short," but, in fact, its approximately 2,200 words far outstrips the average for the Greco-Roman world (87 words!) (Richards, *Paul and First-century Letter Writing*, 163).

10. Ursula K. LeGuin, *The Telling* (New York: Harcourt, 2000), 97-98; emphasis original.

11. See Luke Timothy Johnson, "Imaging the World Scripture Imagines," in *Theology and Scriptural Imagination*, ed. L. Gregory Jones and James J. Buckley (Oxford: Blackwell, 1998), 3-18 (esp. pp. 6-7).

12. Alister E. McGrath, *The Genesis of Doctrine: A Study in the Foundation of Doctrinal Criticism* (Grand Rapids: Eerdmans, 1990), 81.

13. Carl E. Schorske, *Thinking with History: Explorations in the Passage to Modernism* (Princeton, NJ: Princeton University Press, 1998), 3-4.

14. Michael V. Fox, "Bible Scholarship and Faith-Based Study: My View," http://www.sbl-site.org/ Article.aspx?ArticleId=490 (accessed June 5, 2006).

15. Umberto Eco, *Semiotics and the Philosophy of Language* (Bloomington: Indiana University Press, 1984), 103.

16. See Peter Harrison, *The Bible, Protestantism, and the Rise of Natural Science* (Cambridge: Cambridge University Press, 1998); Kenneth J. Howell, *God's Two Books: Copernican Cosmology and Biblical Interpretation in Early Modern Science* (Notre Dame, IN: University of Notre Dame Press, 2002).

17. Cf. Craig Bartholomew, "Post/Late? Modernity as the Context for Christian Scholarship Today," *Themelios* 22, no. 2 (1997): 25-38.

18. See, for example, A. K. M. Adam, ed., *Handbook of Postmodern Biblical Interpretation* (St. Louis: Chalice Press, 2000).

19. I am not sure that the best examples I know actually follow the hermeneutical motto they claim to serve. Exemplary in this regard is Jerry Camery-Hoggatt, *Speaking of God: Reading and Preaching the Word of God* (Peabody, MA: Hendrickson, 1995). Camery-Hoggatt's hermeneutic is well articulated, but his case studies seem less the result of principled bridge-crossing (from ancient text to contemporary context) and more the result of his own well-formed sensibilities and intuition.

20. This is a major emphasis of Stephen E. Fowl and L. Gregory Jones, *Reading in Communion: Scripture and Ethics in Christian Life* (Grand Rapids: Eerdmans, 1991).

21. Pierre Bourdieu, *The Logic of Practice* (Stanford: Stanford University Press, 1980), 53.

22. Cf. Christof Koch, *The Quest for Consciousness: A Neurobiological Approach* (Englewood, CO: Roberts, 2004), 23.

23. Mark Johnson, *The Body in the Mind: The Bodily Basis of Meaning, Imagination, and Reason* (Chicago: University of Chicago Press, 1987), xx.

24. David J. Bryant, *Faith and the Play of Imagination: On the Role of Imagination in Religion*, Studies in American Biblical Hermeneutics 5 (Macon, GA: Mercer University Press, 1989), 5.

25. Owen Flanagan, *The Problem of the Soul: Two Visions of Mind and How to Reconcile Them* (New York: Basic, 2002), 27-55.

26. Cf. Mark Johnson, *Moral Imagination: Implications of Cognitive Science for Ethics* (Chicago: University of Chicago Press, 1993), chap. 8.

27. Recently, for example, Veena Kumari, "Do Psychotherapies Produce Neurobiological Effects?" *Acta Neuropsychiatrica* 18 (2006): 61-70.

28. For example, V. S. Ramachandran, *A Brief Tour of Human Consciousness: From Imposter Poodles to Purple Numbers* (New York: Pi, 2004), chap. 2.

29. See Aaron R. Seitz et al., "Seeing What Is Not There Shows the Costs of Perceptual Learning," *Proceedings of the National Academy of Sciences* 102, no. 25 (June 21, 2005): 9080-85. The importance of "belief" has only begun to be studied empirically; cf., for example, Daniel L. Schacter and Elaine Scarry, eds., *Memory, Brain, and Belief* (Cambridge, MA: Harvard University Press, 2000).

30. Hans-Georg Gadamer, *Truth and Method*, 2nd ed. (New York: Crossroad, 1990).

2. Aims and Assumptions

1. See Christoph Uehlinger, *Weltreich und "eine Rede": Eine neue Deutung der sogenannten Turmbauerzählung (Gen. 11, 1-9)* (Freiburg: Universitätsverlag; Göttingen: Vandenhoeck & Ruprecht, 1990).

2. See Jacques Derrida, "Des tours de Babel," *Semeia* 54 (1991): 3-34 (7).

3. Friedrich Schleiermacher, *The Christian Faith* (Philadelphia: Fortress Press, 1928, 1976), §27.

4. See Bruce D. Marshall, "Christ and the Cultures: The Jewish People and Christian Theology," in *The Cambridge Companion to Christian Doctrine*, ed. Colin E. Gunton (Cambridge: Cambridge University Press, 1997), 81-100 (esp. pp. 82-87); also, Ronald E. Diprose, *Israel and the Development of Christian Thought* (Rome: Istituto Biblico Evangelico Italiano, 2000); R. Kendall Soulen, *The God of Israel and Christian Theology* (Minneapolis: Fortress Press, 1996).

5. Cf. Peter Stuhlmacher, "My Experience with Biblical Theology," in *Biblical Theology: Retrospect and Prospect*, ed. Scott J. Hafemann (Downers Grove, IL: InterVarsity Press, 2002), 174-91 (esp. pp. 176-77).

6. Christopher R. Seitz, "Two Testaments and the Failure of One Tradition-History," in *Biblical Theology: Retrospect and Prospect*, ed. Scott J. Hafemann (Downers Grove, IL: InterVarsity Press, 2002), 195-211 (209).

7. Christopher R. Seitz, *Word without End: The Old Testament as Abiding Theological Witness* (Grand Rapids: Eerdmans, 1998), 45.

8. See, for example, John Goldingay, *Models for Interpretation of Scripture* (Grand Rapids: Eerdmans, 1995), 146-47, 150-51; William L. Schutter, *Hermeneutic and Composition in 1 Peter*, WUNT 2:30 (Tübingen: Mohr Siebeck, 1989), 100-109.

9. See, for example, Francis Watson, "The Old Testament as Christian Scripture: A Response to Professor Seitz," *SJT* 52 (1999): 227-32 (229-30).

10. Bede the Venerable, *Commentary on the Seven Catholic Epistles* (Kalamazoo, MI: Cistercian, 1985), 75-76. How best to render the genitive phrase, "Spirit of Christ," is debated; for the reading I have adopted, see, for example, Paul J. Achtemeier, *1 Peter* (Hermeneia; Minneapolis: Fortress Press, 1996), 109-10.

11. Murray Rae, "Texts in Context: Scripture and the Divine Economy," *JTI*, forthcoming.

12. Cf., for example, Heinz Schürmann, *Das Lukasevangelium*, 2 vols., HTKNT 3 (Freiburg: Herder, 1984–94), 1:573; Joseph A. Fitzmyer, *The Gospel According to Luke*, 2 vols., AB 28-28A (Garden City, NY: Doubleday, 1981–85), 1:814.

13. Similarly, Eduard Schweizer, *The Good News According to Luke* (Atlanta: John Knox Press, 1984): "It is in fact the very revelation of God's 'secrets' (8:10) that leaves them perplexed before the incomprehensible way of God" (p. 163).

14. See Mark L. Strauss, *The Davidic Messiah in Luke-Acts: The Promise and Its Fulfillment in Lukan Christology*, JSNTSup. 110 (Sheffield: Sheffield Academic Press, 1995), 257.

15. This is true of Jew and Gentile alike; see especially Acts 3:17; 17:30.

16. J.-W. Taeger, *Der Mensch und sein Heil: Studien zum Bild des Menschen und zur Sicht der Bekehrung bei Lukas*, SNT 14 (Gütersloh: Gerd Mohn, 1982). Additionally, Taeger failed to account for the plentiful evidence in the Luke narrative of the human need for forgiveness of sins—Luke 1:77; 3:3; 5:20-21, 23-24; 7:47-49; 11:4; 12:10; 17:3-4; 23:34; 24:47; Acts 2:38; 3:19; 5:31; 10:43; 13:38; 15:9; 22:16; 26:18.

17. See Joel B. Green, "The Nature of Conversion in the Acts of the Apostles," in *San Luca Evangelista Testimone Della Fede Che Unisce Atti Del Congresso Internazionale (Padova, 16-21 Ottobre 2000)*, vol. 1, *L'Unità Letteraria e Teologica Dell'opera di Luca*, ed. Giovanni Leonardi and Francesco G. B. Trolese (Padova: Istituto Per La Storia Ecclesiastica Padovana, 2002), 327-34.

18. This point is underscored in Beverly Roberts Gaventa, *From Darkness to Light: Aspects of Conversion in the New Testament* (Philadelphia: Fortress Press, 1986), 52-129.

19. See the helpful discussion in Wayne A. Meeks, *The Origins of Christian Morality: The First Two Centuries* (New Haven: Yale University Press, 1993), 18-36.

20. Peter L. Berger and Thomas Luckmann, *The Social Construction of Reality: A Treatise in the Sociology of Knowledge* (New York: Doubleday, 1966), 160.

21. Robert W. Jenson, "The Religious Power of Scripture," *SJT* 52 (1999): 89-105 (98; italics original).

22. James Wm. McClendon Jr., *Systematic Theology*, vol. 1, *Ethics* (Nashville: Abingdon Press, 1986), 31.

23. Daniel Boyarin, *Intertextuality and the Reading of Midrash* (Bloomington: Indiana University Press, 1990), 16.

24. Paul Ricoeur, *Interpretation Theory: Discourse and the Surplus of Meaning* (Fort Worth: Texas Christian University Press, 1976), 32.

25. For a convenient typology of perspectives in reader-response criticism in New Testament studies, see Kevin J. Vanhoozer, "The Reader in New Testament Interpretation," in *Hearing the New Testament: Strategies for Interpretation*, ed. Joel B. Green (Grand Rapids: Eerdmans, 1995), 301-28.

26. Peter J. Rabinowitz, "Reader-Response Theory and Criticism," in *The Johns Hopkins Guide to Literary Theory and Criticism*, ed. Michael Groden and Martin Kreiswirth (Baltimore: Johns Hopkins University Press, 1994), 606-8.

27. For example, Umberto Eco, *The Role of the Reader: Explorations in the Semiotics of Texts* (Bloomington: Indiana University Press, 1979), 7-11; also, Umberto Eco, *Interpretation and Overinterpretation*, ed. Stefan Collini (Cambridge: Cambridge University Press, 1992).

28. Richard E. Burnett, *Karl Barth's Theological Exegesis: The Hermeneutical Principles of the Römerbrief Period* (Grand Rapids: Eerdmans, 2004).

29. Burnett, *Theological Exegesis*, 101.

30. Karl Barth, *The Epistle to the Romans* (London: Oxford University Press, 1933), 1.

31. Bede, *Commentary on the Seven Catholic Epistles*, 76.

32. Ursula K. LeGuin, *The Telling* (New York: Harcourt, 2000), 97-98.

3. Resources

1. See Joel B. Green and Max Turner, eds., *Between Two Horizons: Spanning New Testament Studies and Systematic Theology* (Grand Rapids: Eerdmans, 2000).

2. See John Sandys-Wunsch and Laurence Eldredge, "J. P. Gabler and the Distinction between Biblical and Dogmatic Theology: Translation, Commentary, and Discussion of His Originality," *SJT* 33 (1980): 133-58. For a recent reassessment of Gabler's work, see Loren T. Stuckenbruck, "Johann Philipp Gabler and the Delineation of Biblical Theology," *SJT* 52 (1999): 139-57.

3. Larry W. Hurtado, "New Testament Studies at the Turn of the Millennium: Questions for the Discipline," *SJT* 52 (1999): 158-78 (170).

4. See, for example, Stephen C. Barton, "New Testament Interpretation as Performance," *SJT* 52 (1999): 179-208; Shannon Craigo-Snell, "Command Performance: Rethinking Performance Interpretation in the Context of *Divine Discourse*," *Modern Theology* 16 (2000): 475-94. Some now prefer other terms, such as *improvisation*, but this appears to be because of a difference of viewpoint regarding the plasticity of the performance metaphor.

5. See Nicholas Wolterstorff, "Living within a Text," in *Faith and Narrative*, ed. Keith E. Yandell (Oxford: Oxford University Press, 2001), 202-13.

6. C. René Padilla, "The Interpreted Word: Reflections on Contextual Hermeneutics," *Themelios* 7, no. 1 (1981): 18-23 (19).

7. Thomas J. Haskell, "Objectivity Is Not Neutrality: Rhetoric Versus Practice in Peter Novick's *That Noble Dream*," in *Objectivity Is Not Neutrality: Explanatory Schemes in History* (Baltimore: Johns Hopkins University Press, 1998), 145-73 (150).

8. Garrett Green, *Theology, Hermeneutics, and Imagination: The Crisis of Interpretation at the End of Modernity* (Cambridge: Cambridge University Press, 2000), 185-86.

9. See above, chapter 2.

10. Alister E. McGrath, *The Genesis of Doctrine: A Study in the Foundation of Doctrinal Criticism* (Grand Rapids: Eerdmans, 1990), esp. pp. 1-13.

11. William J. Abraham, *Canon and Criterion in Christian Theology: From the Fathers to Feminism* (Oxford: Clarendon Press, 1998), 36; emphasis added.

12. John J. O'Keefe and R. R. Reno, *Sanctified Vision: An Introduction to Early Christian Interpretation of the Bible* (Baltimore: Johns Hopkins University Press, 2005), 37.

13. Richard E. Burnett, *Karl Barth's Theological Exegesis: The Hermeneutical Principles of the* Römerbrief *Period* (Grand Rapids: Eerdmans, 2004), 77-78.

14. Luke Timothy Johnson, *The Creed: What Christians Believe and Why It Matters* (New York: Doubleday, 2003), 47.

15. See Jürgen Moltmann, *The Way of Jesus Christ: Christology in Messianic Dimensions* (San Francisco: HarperCollins, 1990), 314-15 (more fully, see pp. 313-41).

16. For example, Romans 3:22; Galatians 2:16; 3:22; Ephesians 3:12; Philippians 3:9; James 2:1; cf. Richard N. Longenecker, "The Foundational Conviction of New Testament Christology: The Obedience/Faithfulness/Sonship of Christ," in *Jesus of Nazareth: Lord and Christ: Essays on the Historical Jesus and New Testament Christology*, ed. Joel B. Green and Max Turner (Grand Rapids: Eerdmans, 1994), 473-88.

17. I refer to "methodists" with a lower-case "m" in order to draw attention to my ecclesial tradition without referring more narrowly to a particular, denominational instantiation of that tradition.

18. John Wesley, "Advice to the People Called Methodists with Regard to Dress," §5.1. More generally, see, for example, Scott J. Jones, *John Wesley's Conception and Use of Scripture* (Nashville: Kingswood Books, 1995); Thomas C. Oden, *John Wesley's Scriptural Christianity: A Plain Exposition of His Teaching on Christian Doctrine* (Grand Rapids: Zondervan, 1994), 55-65; Mack B. Stokes, *The Bible in the Wesleyan Heritage* (Nashville: Abingdon Press, 1979).

19. John Wesley, "On God's Vineyard," §1.1, in *the Works of John Wesley*, vol. 3, ed. Albert C. Outler (Nashville: Abingdon Press, 1986), 504.

20. John Wesley, "Further Thoughts on Christian Perfection," in *the Works of John Wesley*, 3rd ed., vol. 11 (Grand Rapids: Baker, 1979), 429. For this emphasis on Wesley, see, for example, Oden, *Scriptural Christianity*, 57-58; and especially Jones, *Scripture*, 114-23.

21. Kenneth J. Collins, *The Theology of John Wesley: Holy Love and the Shape of Grace* (Nashville: Abingdon Press, 2007).

22. John Wesley, preface to "Sermons on Several Occasions," §5, in *The Works of John Wesley*, vol. 1, ed. Albert C. Outler (Nashville: Abingdon Press, 1984), 105-6.

23. I have borrowed this definition of "theme" from Gerald Prince, *Narrative as Theme: Studies in French Fiction* (Lincoln: University of Nebraska Press, 1992).

24. See, for example, Hazard Adams, introduction to *Critical Theory Since Plato*, rev. ed. (Fort Worth: Harcourt Brace Jovanovich, 1992), 1-9; also M. H. Abrams, *The Mirror and the Lamp: Romantic Theory and the Critical Tradition* (Oxford: Oxford University Press, 1953).

25. See Pui-lan Kwok, *Discovering the Bible in the Non-biblical World* (Maryknoll, NY: Orbis, 1995).

26. Gerald West, *Biblical Hermeneutics of Liberation: Modes of Reading the Bible in the South African Context*, 2nd ed. (Maryknoll, NY: Orbis, 1995).

27. See Kevin J. Vanhoozer, "Hyperactive Hermeneutics: Is the Bible Being Overinterpreted?" *Catalyst* 19, no. 4 (1992): 3-4.

28. Hans-Georg Gadamer, *Truth and Method*, 2nd ed. (New York: Crossroad, 1990), 269.

29. Charles Taylor, *Sources of the Self: The Making of the Modern Identity* (Cambridge, MA: Harvard University Press, 1989).

30. Henri de Lubac, *Scripture in the Tradition* (New York: Crossroad, 2000), 152-53.

31. Cf. Christopher Bryan, *And God Spoke: The Authority of the Bible for the Church Today* (Cambridge, MA: Cowley, 2002), 17-21.

32. Thomas C. Oden, ed., *Ancient Christian Commentary on Scripture* (Downers Grove, IL: InterVarsity Press, ongoing series); Robert Louis Wilken, ed., *The Church's Bible* (Grand Rapids: Eerdmans, ongoing series); Daniel M. Patte, ed., *Global Bible Commentary* (Nashville: Abingdon Press, 2004).

33. For recent discussion, see, for example, Stephen R. Holmes, *Listening to the Past: The Place of Tradition in Theology* (Grand Rapids: Baker Academic, 2002).

34. D. H. Williams, *Evangelicals and Tradition: The Formative Influence of the Early Church* (Grand Rapids: Baker Academic, 2005), 101.

4. Methods

1. To admit that these differences raised questions is not the same thing as suggesting that they were the source of angst among early Christians. To the contrary, the early church as a whole resisted any movement toward embracing a single narrative of Jesus' life and mission over against the others, and was not drawn to an early attempt at a "harmony of the Gospels" (Tatian's *Diatesseron*). In fact, second-century theologians put forward sometimes ingenious rationales for the existence of four authoritative gospel narratives (Irenaeus) and spoke of multiple witnesses to the one gospel, who was Jesus Christ (Justin Martyr).

2. On developments in the philosophy of history, see, for example, Ernst Breisach, *Historiography: Ancient, Medieval, and Modern*, 2nd ed. (Chicago: University of Chicago Press, 1994).

3. John Dominic Crossan observed that "*historical Jesus research* is becoming something of a scholarly bad joke . . . a very safe place to do theology and call it history, to do autobiography and call it biography" (*The Historical Jesus: The Life of a Mediterranean Jewish Peasant* [San Francisco: HarperSanFrancisco, 1991], xxvii-iii); inexplicably, having made this statement, he went on to write his own, massive, "life of Jesus." For one of the most helpful and successful critiques of the whole enterprise, see Luke Timothy Johnson, *The Real Jesus: The Misguided Quest for the Historical Jesus and the Truth of the Traditional Gospels* (San Francisco: HarperSanFrancisco, 1996). For issues related to the philosophy of history as these might relate to Jesus studies, see Scot McKnight, *Jesus and His Death: Historiography, the Historical Jesus, and Atonement Theory* (Waco, TX: Baylor University Press, 2005), 3-46; also Joel B. Green, "In Quest of the Historical: Jesus, the Gospels, and Historicisms Old and New," *CSR* 28 (1999): 544-60.

4. See, for example, David Lowenthal, *The Past Is a Foreign Country* (Cambridge: Cambridge University Press, 1985); Hayden White, *The Content of the Form: Narrative Discourse and Historical Representation* (Baltimore: Johns Hopkins University Press, 1987); Albert Cook, *History/Writing: The Theory and Practice of History in Antiquity and in Modern Times* (Cambridge: Cambridge University Press, 1988).

5. See, for example, James Phelan, *Narrative as Rhetoric: Technique, Audiences, Ethics, Ideology* (Columbus: Ohio State University Press, 1996).

6. Recently, for example, Louise J. Lawrence, *Reading with Anthropology: Exhibiting Aspects of New Testament Religion* (Milton Keynes: Paternoster, 2005); for an introductory survey, see Howard Clark Kee, *Knowing the Truth: A Sociological Approach to New Testament Interpretation* (Minneapolis: Fortress Press, 1989).

7. Umberto Eco, *The Role of the Reader: Explorations in the Semiotics of Texts* (Bloomington: Indiana University Press, 1979), 3-4, 37 (citing Lévi-Strauss in an interview with Paolo Caruso in *Paese sera-Libri* [January 20, 1967], reprinted in *Conversazioni con Lévi-Strauss, Foucault, Lacan*, ed. Paolo Caruso [Milan: Mursia, 1969]).

8. See Stephen Greenblatt, "Culture," in *Critical Terms for Literary Study*, ed. Frank Lentricchia and Thomas McLaughlin (Chicago: University of Chicago Press, 1990), 225-32.

9. See, for example, Wolfgang Iser, *The Implied Reader: Patterns of Communication in Prose Fiction from Bunyan to Beckett* (Baltimore: Johns Hopkins University Press, 1974); Eco, *Role of the Reader*; Umberto Eco, *The Limits of Interpretation* (Indianapolis: Indiana University Press, 1990).

10. For an exemplar of this sort of cross-cultural engagement, see Khiok-Khng (K. K.) Yeo, *What Has Jerusalem to Do with Beijing? Biblical Interpretation from a Chinese Perspective* (Harrisburg, PA: Trinity Press, 1998).

11. More fully, see Cain Hope Felder, ed., *Stony the Road We Trod: African American Biblical Interpretation* (Minneapolis: Fortress Press, 1991).

12. On Latino/Latina interpretation, see the overview of Justo L. González, *Santa Biblia: The Bible through Hispanic Eyes* (Nashville: Abingdon Press, 1996).

13. For examples, see Stanley P. Saunders, "Revelation and Resistance: Narrative and Worship in John's Apocalypse," in *Narrative Reading, Narrative Preaching: Reuniting New Testament Interpretation and Proclamation*, ed. Joel B. Green and Michael Pasquarello III (Grand Rapids: Baker Academic, 2003), 117-50; and Joel B. Green, *1 Peter*, Two Horizons Commentary on the New Testament (Grand Rapids: Eerdmans, 2007).

14. See, for example, John R. Donahue, "Modern and Postmodern Critical Methods of Biblical Study," in *Scripture: An Ecumenical Introduction to the Bible and Its Interpretation*, ed. Michael J. Gorman (Peabody, MA: Hendrickson, 2005), 147-62; even more widely, Janice Chapel Anderson and Stephen D. Moore, eds., *Mark and Method: New Approaches in Biblical Studies* (Minneapolis: Fortress Press, 1991); Joel B. Green, ed., *Hearing the New Testament: Strategies for Interpretation* (Grand Rapids: Eerdmans, 1995).

15. Gillian Brown and George Yule, *Discourse Analysis* (Cambridge: Cambridge University Press, 1983), 234-36.

16. Jan Blommaert, *Discourse: A Critical Introduction* (Cambridge: Cambridge University Press, 2005), 47.

17. I will return to the question of "meaning," briefly, in chapter 5.

18. I have expanded these first two points from the criteria of validity outlined in Sandra Schneiders, *The Revelatory Text: Interpreting the New Testament as Sacred Scripture* (San Francisco: HarperCollins 1991), 165-67.

19. Alasdair MacIntyre, *Three Rival Versions of Moral Inquiry: Encyclopaedia, Genealogy and Tradition* (Notre Dame, IN: University of Notre Dame Press, 1990), 65-66.

20. Paul Ricoeur, *Interpretation Theory: Discourse and the Surplus of Meaning* (Fort Worth: Texas Christian University Press, 1976), 32.

5. Authority

1. As in chapter 3, I refer to "methodist" with a lower-case "m" in order to draw attention to my ecclesial tradition without referring more narrowly to a particular, denominational instantiation of that tradition.

2. Scott J. Jones, *John Wesley's Conception and Use of Scripture* (Nashville: Kingswood Books, 1995).

3. Mack Stokes, *The Bible in the Wesleyan Heritage* (Nashville: Abingdon Press, 1979), 15.

4. See Jones, *John Wesley's Conception.*

5. For criticism of the Quadrilateral as an expression of Wesley and methodism, see, for example, Ted A. Campbell, "The 'Wesleyan Quadrilateral': The Story of a Modern Methodist Myth," in *Doctrine and Theology in The United Methodist Church*, ed. Thomas A. Langford (Nashville: Abingdon Press, 1991), 154-61; Scott J. Jones, "John Wesley on the Authority and Interpretation of Scripture," *Catalyst* 19, no. 1 (1992): 2, 6; Stephen Gunter et al., *Wesley and the Quadrilateral: Renewing the Conversation* (Nashville: Abingdon Press, 1997). From outside the Wesleyan tradition, see, for example, Donald G. Bloesch, *A Theology of Word and Spirit: Authority and Method in Theology* (Downers Grove: InterVarsity Press, 1992), 208-11; H. Darrell Lance, "Response to 'The Bible and Human Sexuality,'" *American Baptist Quarterly* 12 (1993): 323-28 (327).

6. Robert Wuthnow, *Acts of Compassion: Caring for Others and Helping Ourselves* (Princeton, NJ: Princeton University Press, 1991), chap. 6.

7. See the helpful essay by Robert N. Bellah, "The Recovery of Biblical Language in American Life," *Radix Magazine* 18, no. 4 (1988): 4-7, 29-31.

8. Gallup estimates that three out of ten Americans believe the Bible is the actual word of God (Frank Newport, "Twenty-Eight Percent Believe Bible Is Actual Word of God," http://poll.gallup.com/content/?ci=22885 [accessed June 23, 2006]). With a population of almost 300 million, this puts the number of persons who share this belief in the neighborhood of 100 million. Admittedly, this is a crude way of measuring the pervasiveness of a belief in biblical authority, since others might credit the Bible as authoritative Scripture without thinking of it in terms of "the actual word of God," a phrase that is fraught with serious ambiguities.

9. Although there is significant latitude in how these two terms are defined, these are representative. I have taken them from J. I. Packer, "Infallibility and Inerrancy of the Bible," in *New Dictionary of Theology*, ed. Sinclair B. Ferguson and David F. Wright (Downers Grove, IL: InterVarsity Press, 1988), 337-39 (337). For greater nuance, see the older but still useful typology in Robert K. Johnson,

Evangelicals at an Impasse: Biblical Authority in Practice (Atlanta: John Knox Press, 1979), 15-47.

10. We can name famous counterexamples, of course, persons who came to Christian faith as a result of their critical, intellectual quest to test its "truth" (e.g., C. S. Lewis or Frank Morison).

11. Cf. John Goldingay, *Models for Scripture* (Grand Rapids: Eerdmans, 1994), 194-96.

12. See Hans-Georg Gadamer, *Truth and Method*, 2nd ed. (New York: Crossroad, 2000); E. D. Hirsch Jr., *Validity in Interpretation* (New Haven: Yale University Press, 1967); Paul Ricoeur, *Interpretation Theory: Discourse and the Surplus of Meaning* (Fort Worth: Texas Christian University Press, 1976); Paul Ricoeur, *The Conflict of Interpretations: Essays in Hermeneutics*, ed. Don Ihde (Evanston, IL: Northwestern University Press, 1974); Kevin J. Vanhoozer, *Is There a Meaning in This Text? The Bible, the Reader, and the Morality of Literary Knowledge* (Grand Rapids: Zondervan, 1998). For overview, see, for example, Robert C. Holub, "Hermeneutics: Twentieth Century," in *The Johns Hopkins Guide to Literary Theory and Criticism*, ed. Michael Groden and Martin Kreiswirth (Baltimore: Johns Hopkins University Press, 1994), 379-82.

13. For details, see Joel B. Green, "Crucifixion," in *Cambridge Companion to Jesus*, ed. Markus Bockmuehl (Cambridge: Cambridge University Press, 2001), 87-101.

14. Karl Barth, "The Strange New World within the Bible," in *The Word of God and the Word of Man* (Gloucester: Peter Smith, 1978), 28-50 (28).

15. Barth, "Strange New World," 33, 43, 45.

16. Charles Taylor, *Sources of the Self: The Making of the Modern Identity* (Cambridge, MA: Harvard University Press, 1989).

17. Robert N. Bellah et al., *Habits of the Heart: Individualism and Commitment in American Life* (Berkeley: University of California Press, 1985); see Robert N. Bellah et al., eds., *Individualism and Commitment in American Life: Readings on the Themes of Habits of the Heart* (San Francisco: Harper & Row, 1987).

18. For example, C. H. Reynolds and R. V. Norman, eds., *Community in America: The Challenge of Habits of the Heart* (Berkeley: University of California Press, 1988).

19. Cf., for example, Suzanne Gordon, *Prisoners of Men's Dreams: Striking Out for a New Feminine Future* (Boston: Little, Brown, 1991).

20. See Robert Wuthnow, *Sharing the Journey: Support Groups and America's New Quest for Community* (New York: Free Press, 1994).

21. See Robert A. Di Vito, "Old Testament Anthropology and the Construction of Personal Identity," *CBQ* 61 (1999): 217-38.

22. Horst Dietrich Preuss, *Old Testament Theology*, 2 vols. (Louisville: Westminster John Knox Press, 1996), 2:171.

23. John Wesley, preface to *Sermons on Several Occasions*, §5, *The Works of John Wesley*, vol. 1, ed. Albert C. Outler (Nashville: Abingdon Press, 1984), 105-6.

24. Goldingay, *Models for Scripture*, 121.

25. John Goldingay, "Biblical Narrative and Systematic Theology," in *Between*

Two Horizons: Spanning New Testament Studies and Systematic Theology, ed. Joel B. Green and Max Turner (Grand Rapids: Eerdmans, 2000), 123-42 (131).

26. Cf. Richard Bauckham, "Reading Scripture as a Coherent Story," in *The Art of Reading Scripture*, ed. Ellen F. Davis and Richard B. Hays (Grand Rapids: Eerdmans, 2003), 38-53.

27. Philip F. Esler, *Galatians* (London: Routledge, 1998), 5.

28. Philip F. Esler, "Introduction: Models, Contexts, and Kerygma in New Testament Interpretation," in *Modelling Early Christianity: Social-scientific Studies of the New Testament in Its Context*, ed. Philip F. Esler (London: Routledge, 1995), 1-20 (18).

29. James D. G. Dunn, *Christianity in the Making*, vol. 1, *Jesus Remembered* (Grand Rapids: Eerdmans, 2003), 94.

30. George Lindbeck, *The Nature of Doctrine: Religion and Theology in a Postliberal Age* (Louisville: Westminster John Knox Press, 1984).

31. Cf., for example, Hayden White, *The Content of the Form: Narrative Discourse and Historical Representation* (Baltimore: Johns Hopkins University Press, 1987).

32. Cf., for example, Jonathan A. Carter, "Telling Times: History, Emplotment, and Truth," *History and Theory* 42 (2003): 1-27.

33. James Phelan, *Narrative as Rhetoric: Technique, Audiences, Ethics, Ideology* (Columbus: Ohio State University Press, 1996), 17.

34. Ibid., 4.

35. Trevor Hart, *Faith Thinking: The Dynamics of Christian Theology* (Downers Grove, IL: InterVarsity Press, 1995), 143.

36. Ibid., 161-62.

CPSIA information can be obtained at www.ICGtesting.com
Printed in the USA
267085BV00004B/62/P